MW00974013

HOW TO RAISE
SUCCESSFUL
CHILDREN

By

Joe Wilkins

Wilkins Information Systems

How To Raise Successful Children. Copyright © 2011 by Joe H. Wilkins, Jr. All rights reserved. Printed and formatted in the United States of America. No part of this book may be used or reproduced in any manner whatsoever without written permission except in the case of brief quotations included in critical articles and reviews. For further information write to Wilkins Information Systems, 5544 Stonehaven Drive, Stone Mountain, Georgia, 30087-5793.

First Edition

Copyright © 2012 Joe Wilkins

All rights reserved.

ISBN: 146626327X

ISBN-13: 9781466263277

CONTENTS

ACKNOWLEDGMENTS

A lot of people have contributed to and been a part of the evolution of this book—often in ways of which they are not aware. I want to give special thanks to my wife, Lorela Nichols Wilkins, and my children, Deirdre Wilkins Ritger and Darrick Wilkins. I also wish to thank, in alphabetical order, the following people:

All my Air Force colleagues (1955–1959); Elaine and Ed Boeckman; Lisa and Rick Burris; Gary Cabbage, M.Ed.; Al Daly, M.Div.; the Dekalb Addiction Clinic staff; John Dixon, M.Div., M.Ed.; Sandy and Dean Ericson; members of the Evangelical Lutheran Church of the Redeemer in Atlanta, Georgia; the Georgia Division of Rehabilitation Services; the Georgia Licensed Professional Counselors Association; the staff at the Georgia Mental Health Institute; Travis Godbee, M.Div., M.Ed.; Harold Haddle, Ph.D.; Alexander Halkos, M.D.; Mary and Austin Hinely; Ben Hogan; Ellie and Ed Kohler; Sadie and Charlie Kornegay; Dorothy Jaeger Lee,

M.D.; Robert E. Lee, D.D.; Raphael Levine, M.D.; the staff and volunteers at Lutheran Services of Georgia; Chip Lynch; Billie and Jack Massey; Suzie Massey; Kenneth Matheny, Ph.D.; McKinley Tech High School schoolmates and teachers; George Moore, Ph.D.; all my golfing friends at Mystery Valley; Juanita and Guy Nichols; all my wife's Nichols and Dawkins relatives; schoolmates and teachers of Palatka, Florida Senior High School; Amy Parker and Frank Pritchard; Chris Ritger, MBA; Joan and Dave Ritger; Ernest Robinson, Ph.D.; Lois and Harold Skillrud, D.D.; Nicholas L. Smith; Stanley Smits, Ph.D.; Joye and Mack Spates; Gail and Barry Spurlock; Stepping Stone Rehabilitation Residence; Paul Susko, M.Ed.; Janet and David Wilkins; Joe H. Wilkins, Sr.; Nora and Joseph S. Wilkins; all my Wilkins relatives; and Dorothy and Hank Wohlgemuth, M.Div.

FORWARD

Why another book on child rearing when there are so many good ones out there already? Many parents have told me that many of the books are too clinical and detailed for their modern, busy lives. Modern, fast-changing times have made us throw out some of the old techniques because they just don't fit the situations our children find themselves in these days. It's a sad fact that most people raise their children using the techniques of long ago. Also, many of the newer child-rearing techniques that have been developed by child psychologists in structured settings often don't transfer over well into our everyday lives. I have attempted to make this book a modern guide to deal with the child-rearing problems of today.

However, don't think me totally disdainful of other people's work in this area. Almost all writings about child rearing have some positive things from which you can benefit. But temper all of them with a bit of common sense.

This book was spurred by the fact that, over the years in my counseling practice, I noticed that recent generations seemed to be lacking many qualities that are essential in coping with an ever-changing, highly evolving, technological world. And it is clear that if our children are going to make it, they need to be competent in areas that you and I didn't even have to think about.

I often think about a person who had a great deal of influence on my childhood: my grandfather, Joseph S. Wilkins. Here was a man born in 1874 in eastern Tennessee. He was basically a farmer all his life, but he also taught some school and dabbled in real estate. Soon after marrying my grandmother at the age of thirty-one, he looked out on the declining fertility of his Tennessee farm and didn't like what he saw. Also echoing in his mind was Horace Greeley's advice: "Go West, young man!"

And that's what he did. In the early 1900s, he packed up his pregnant wife and all their belongings in a Conestoga wagon and headed west, eventually homesteading on free federal land in southwest Colorado. Their first child was born during the journey. After certifying his claim, he built a sod-dugout home and began farming on the rich soil of the prairie. Needless to say, Granddad was adventurous and a risk taker.

However, sad to say, after a few years on the lonely, desolate prairie, living in his crude home, miles from their nearest neighbor, Grandmama became ill with a "heart condition," probably from the harshness and loneliness of their lives. A doctor told Granddad to get her back east for her health.

So back to Tennessee they went, giving up the farm at considerable financial sacrifice and demonstrating compassion, responsibility, and good sense on Granddad's part.

Back in Tennessee, he and Grandmama had five more children. Life was not easy, but they did okay because Granddad was responsible, industrious, hardworking, clever, and had good social skills. And they knew, from good intuition and personal experience from their own upbringing, how to teach their six children what they needed to succeed in life.

Then, in 1930, he received a letter from his brother in Leesburg, Florida, who had been in the real estate business there since the 1890s. His brother asked him to come to Florida and join him in his business. The circumstances were ripe, so Granddad packed up his family and moved down to Leesburg, Florida, in hopes of improving the family's fortunes.

The Depression set in hard about that time, but it didn't seem to bother Granddad at all. When the real estate market fizzled out, he bought an orange grove, then a gas station, rented land, and grew watermelons and peanuts. He bought a large rooming house and rented rooms to transient workers. He did most of the physical labor himself, with help from his children. He did whatever he had to do to support his family. In his spare time, he went fishing and beat most of his friends at checkers and shuffleboard.

Granddad provided well for his family, but they were not rich or well-to-do by any means. There was little spare money, but he managed what he had well and taught his children how to do the same. But you would never have guessed their modest financial condition by the success of their six children: They all went to college and married well. The oldest daughter, Okemah, graduated with a master's degree in Home Economics and taught school until retirement. The next child, Juanita, earned a master's degree in nutrition, was commissioned a lieutenant in the Women's Army Corps in World War II, and also taught school until she retired. My father, Joe Wilkins, Sr., earned a master's degree in entomology and worked for the Federal Farm Security Administration, later becoming a salesman until retirement. The next child, Roe Wilkins, earned a law degree and was a captain in the 101st Airborne Division, surviving the Normandy Invasion and the Battle of the Bulge, and later became a very successful attorney in Orlando. The last son, Raymond Wilkins, served as an enlisted man in the Army in World War II, got a degree in electrical engineering after the war, and worked the rest of his life with NASA at Cape Canaveral in the space program. The youngest child, Ophelia, went to college for two years, studying music, but gave up a promising career to get married and raise a successful family.

How, you may ask, did my grandparents manage to raise such a successful family during such hard national times as the Depression and World War II? Not only did they succeed with their six children, but all eleven of their grandchildren did well and achieved similar goals, as have the great-grandchildren. And not one of them has an alcohol or drug problem, has ever been locked up in jail, or been on welfare!

Stopping to reflect on all this suggests this is quite an achievement for one family. And the success is rolling on to this day. But the Wilkins family is not unique in this respect, because many families and individuals in America have done just as well. How did they do it? That's what this book is about.

Granddad lived ninety years, dying in 1964. In his lifetime he saw the transition of America from horse-drawn farm equipment and wagons to tractors and automobiles. He witnessed the electrification of our cities and farms. He saw the invention of motion pictures, radio, and television. Just after he returned to Tennessee from Colorado, the Wright brothers flew the first airplane. Then he witnessed the development of faster airplanes and jets. He saw rockets leap into space. He saw the development of penicillin, polio, and other vaccines for diseases that had crippled or killed many people he knew. He lived through the Spanish American War, World War I, World War II, the Korean War, the Cold War, and Vietnam. In short, he saw so many changes over his life of ninety short years that one might wonder how he managed to cope with all this.

The answer, of course, is his parents, who did it by instinct and family tradition, raised him to be a successful person, and he intuitively repeated the cycle with his own children. For example, he pounded into the heads of all his children from day one the Wilkins family tradition that education was the main key to a successful life and that all his children *were* going to college, Great Depression be damned! Thus, the children grew up with the fixed notion that they *would* go to college—even though there really wasn't sufficient money for it. And there weren't many scholarships or grants in those days.

How did they do it? Basically, they were taught the principles described in this book, and they put them into action. They worked their way through college by doing whatever jobs they could get. Then, when the oldest ones finished, they helped the younger ones. Thus, the whole family pulled themselves up by their bootstraps, with Granddad helping them as much as he could. And I was blessed to be born into such a successful family. My wife's family has a similar story, proving that success breeds success, and it can be carried on in your family if you know how to do it.

But in today's world, family systems are not as stable and extended as they used to be, and the modern nuclear family seems more alone and fragmented than ever. Before, we could rely on custom and tradition and social systems that were more stable. Today's parents have to rely increasingly on their own wits and education, with the extended family no longer there to help. But the demands of modern living and survival leave little time to do a quality job with our children, giving most parents a vague sense of unease that they are not raising their children in an optimum manner.

You, the reader, may be a descendant of a successful family, and naturally you want to pass this on to your children, but you know you can't do it the way your mother and father or grandparents did, because times have changed, and it's a faster-paced and sometimes harsher world. So new techniques are needed.

The saving grace about us humans, though, is, even if we don't come from the best background, we can learn what we need if we set our efforts to it. And that's what this book is all about.

Now, let's get started!

(For more about the author, see his resume in the appendix.)

CHAPTER 1

THE SUCCESSFUL CHILD

Just what is a successful child? And what is it that leads a child to become a successful adult? As a general rule, we all know that if we raise our children properly, they will usually turn out okay as adults. I say *usually* because that's not always true. We all are aware of adults who came from so-called "good" families, but who turned out badly in some ways. Examples are Kenneth Lay of Enron, Bernie Elbers of World Com, Martha Stewart, Richard Nixon, and Bill Clinton, all of whom were successful in many ways, yet they had character flaws that caused them serious problems in life—problems that could have possibly been avoided if certain key values had been firmly instilled in them as children.

Some will argue that these *are* successful people—but some will say they're not, depending on one's "worldview." Such disagreements just show that we need to be careful in defining "successful people."

So, let's attempt a definition of successful adults and then work backward to their childhoods to see how they achieved such success.

Successful people are those who have their total world in reasonably good order, such that they are appropriately getting their needs met in a manner that leads them to be happy and satisfied—in concert with the conventions, laws, and rules of the society in which they live. Further, these people are capable of earning/securing enough money to meet all or most of their needs and desires, and can do so without depriving, cheating, or hurting others (1).

Thus, by inference, successful people obey the laws of their society and do not lie, cheat, or steal. Successful people have good manners and try to follow the Golden Rule by treating others as they would like to be treated. To the extent that people do not follow the Golden Rule, then they are automatically doomed to a type of social hypocrisy, in that they will have, to a certain degree, removed themselves from their community's agreed-upon code of behavior that promotes the common good. Adherence to the Golden Rule gives successful people a sense of duty to one's community, state, nation, and planet, and helps them cut through a lot social chaff during difficult decision-making times.

Further, successful people have developed some idea about what happens after they die. Whether we like it or not, we all must face the "Grim Reaper" someday, and people who don't prepare properly for their own deaths often live disconnected, psychologically confused lives—especially as they get older (2).

A colleague of mine once told me that a successful child is one that is not in jail, not on illegal drugs, doesn't drink irresponsibly, doesn't smoke, has a job, has fathered no illegitimate children, and isn't still living with his parents!

He wasn't too far off the mark, in my opinion.

It is clear that some of our past ideas of successful people need to be redefined. One only needs to look around our world at some of the people who are lionized and adulated in the media to realize that notoriety is often substituted for success. While some people are very successful in their careers (for example, making enormous amounts of money and achieving extensive fame), many of these folks fail miserably at home or in other areas of life. Bill Clinton was a very successful politician, having achieved the pinnacle of accomplishment in rising to the U.S. presidency, yet he was a failure in the management of his sex life and had to endure the consequent negative effects on his relationships with the U.S. Congress, his wife and daughter, and a huge part of the American public. John F. Kennedy was a successful president, senator, writer, and war hero, yet he was a womanizer and adulterer. Jane Fonda was a very successful actress, yet presumed that her success on the screen made her an international expert on issues of war and national policy. Martin Luther King, Jr. was a successful preacher/orator and civil rights activist, but was unable to follow the tenants of his own religion regarding sexual activity outside of marriage. Baseball hero Joe DiMaggio was held up to the public for years as a model sports personality, yet after his death we learn that, in his personal life, he was a selfish, arrogant, greedy man. Elizabeth Taylor was a beautiful, wonderful actress, but did not have a clue as to how to pick a proper husband, as eight marriages will testify.

With these people, one only needs to look back into their childhoods and examine their upbringing—or lack thereof—to see the chains of cause and effect that led to some of their critical flaws as adults. However, a word of caution needs to be raised at this point: We cannot always blame all human flaws on "bad" upbringing. At times, we humans can choose to engage in misdeeds in spite of dedicated parental supervision. We all have free wills, and as most religions note, we're all sinners. However, it is my belief and experience that children who have had positive parental guidance are much more likely to grow into the type of adults we would desire.

This is not to say that we're seeking to raise "perfect" children, because that's not possible. And many readers may take me to task with my above examples of unsuccessful adults. Oftentimes, such judgments are strongly influenced by the values held by the judge, which is certainly true in my case. And you can certainly rattle off the names of some *really* unsuccessful people, such as Saddam Hussein, Osama bin Laden, Josef Stalin, Adolf Hitler, and the like. All of this only illustrates that this whole business of raising successful children is somewhat a relative matter, and you, dear reader, have to decide where you stand—relatively speaking!

But we can't let matters of relativity freeze our brains and deter us parents from doing the best we can with our children. We all want to maximize their opportunities to live out their lives in a happy, responsible manner.

In the chapters that follow, we will be examining fifteen areas that are essential to successful child rearing, to which parents should attend so that their children are started out on pathways that will maximize their chances of developing into adults of whom they can be proud.

The areas we will be examining are outlined on the contents page of this book. You do not have to read them in order. I suggest you study them in order of importance to you. Initially, all this may seem like a daunting task—and raising children is not easy—but it's not nuclear science, either. As parents, you will be using your own intelligence, experience, skills, schools, family resources, church, sports, media, leisure activities, and community to help you with this process. And I am asserting emphatically that raising your children is the most important and meaningful job you will ever have.

As parents, you will watch and monitor your children, as well as keep a careful eye on others with whom they are involved. And you *will* be successful if you work at it in an informed and attentive manner.

CHAPTER 2

STARTING OUT IN INFANCY

Raising a successful child begins when you bring that infant home from the hospital. Of course, you will be happy and overjoyed to have such a beautiful, happy, adored baby. Relatives, friends, and neighbors will shower your newborn with gifts and adulation. And that's good.

Now, the hard work begins.

It goes without saying that when you have children, your needs should take a backseat to theirs. Before you now is a helpless, crying, gurgling, cooing, beautiful little baby that can do nothing for itself—except cry when something's not right in its little, limited world. And it's your duty to address these crying episodes, because when babies cry, it means that something is not right. They're probably hungry or hurting, and since they can't talk yet, all they can do is cry to let you know that you need to attend to them. And it's your job to figure what's wrong and fix it.

It is not the purpose of this book to go into a lot of detail about the physical needs of your baby. Many good books have been written on this subject. But your pediatrician should be your primary source of information. However, the most frequent things that make babies cry are hunger, intestinal gas, wetness, dirty diapers, diaper rash, abrupt loud noises, loneliness, and the desire to be picked up and cuddled (1).

Please remember this: *You can't spoil infants!* You can't hold, cuddle, and comfort them too much (2). I recall an interview on television years ago with jazz musician Duke Ellington. He was asked why he was always so calm and relaxed and never seemed to lose his temper. His reply was, "Because my feet didn't hit the ground until I was five years old!" He explained further that he was always being picked up and cuddled by his mother and other relatives, getting all the nurture he needed!

Lots of holding, comforting, and proper feeding are what instill a positive self-image in babies. With caring, attentive parents, infants' emotional systems begin to develop in a positive direction. At the pre-language level, they then begin to perceive that this is a good, caring, comfortable world, and everything's okay. What's more, whenever they cry, and someone attends to them, they begin to *feel*, at a subconscious level, that they have some power and influence over their small world (3). (Might it be that the song "It's a Small World" is alluding to this?)

These infantile feelings of *comfort* later expand in infants' psyche into feelings of *confidence*, which later in life serve them well when they're trying to accomplish those lofty goals to which they may aspire. Conversely, if they cry and cry, and no one attends to them by picking them up, consoling them, and tending to their needs, they will gradually "learn" that, since no one pays attention to them, they must not be worth much, so what's the use in trying? Children who enter adulthood with this later "worldview" are very prone to becoming chronic underachievers. They will often give up on tasks prematurely and fail, thus confirming those negative lessons programmed into their emotional systems as an infants. And they will repeat this self-defeating cycle over and over again throughout their lifetimes (4).

Some parents have been taught that you have to be careful not to spoil infants. No less than an authority than the U.S. Department of Agriculture in the 1930s was promoting this philosophy in their literature that was distributed throughout the country. We can only speculate how many children were emotionally crippled by this "sage" advice from the federal government (5).

Betty was a very conscientious mother and she had her first child in the 1930s. Being an orphan, she was rather sketchy on child-rearing techniques, so she obtained the latest "scientific" information on child rearing from the aforementioned U.S. Department of Agriculture, in the form of their brochures, upon the advice of her obstetrician! These brochures told her to feed the baby *on the mother's schedule*, then put the baby to bed in the early evening in a cool room and shut the door. The mother was not to go back in, even if the baby started crying. (After all, we didn't want to "spoil" the baby!) The baby had to learn that the world didn't revolve around her. And that, dear readers, was how she raised her daughter. However, several aunts of the baby were around from time to time, and they reported that they would sneak into the room, unknown to the mother, and pick up the baby and sooth her by talking softly and rocking her. Perhaps that's why this baby didn't lapse into total neuroticism as an adult (6)!

I repeat, you cannot spoil infants! Why? Because they are totally helpless and need constant care. For those parents who have to place their babies in day care centers or hire nannies to tend them while they work, they need to make sure their caregivers tend to the children when they cry. And check on these people to make sure they're doing what else you ask of them.

Having said all this, you *can* spoil children after they leave infancy and enter toddlerhood. Many parents are good at catering to their infants' every need—but they don't know when to stop! And, you may ask, when is the proper time to begin letting children do things for themselves? Obviously, the answer is when they're able! As children develop their abilities, let them try these new behaviors. Let them feed themselves—even if it is messy at first. You can gradually teach them how to be neat in their eating. If they want to crawl, and later walk and run, let them, within the confines of safety, of course. But don't let your fears that they might hurt themselves keep you from letting them "spread their wings." Do not overly stifle their freedom of play and movement. Take reasonable precautions by "child-proofing" (making safe) their play areas, but let them go! When children do things for themselves, they're developing self-confidence.

Over the years, I've had several adult clients who we counselors referred to as "mama's boys or girls." When I checked into their backgrounds, in almost all cases, they were held back by their mothers—and sometimes fathers—and not allowed reasonable freedom as toddlers, usually because of fears that they would get hurt; consequently, they were overprotected. This led to them either being chronically angry at the world or very passive and unsure about their behavior. Many of them turned to alcohol and drugs in their teens or adulthood to compensate.

Holding, cuddling, kissing, and hugging—you can't do too much of this for the first couple of years or so. Extensive psychological research has shown that children who don't get these "soft fuzzies" grow up to be fearful, distractible, inattentive, suspicious adults. They don't trust themselves or others. It's as if the world is a scary, hostile place and they must be constantly on guard to prevent being hurt (7).

As your infants become toddlers, and later, young children, they'll let you know when to back off on the excessive touchy-feely, lovey-dovey stuff. They usually do it by rejecting your advances to rush off to other interests-of-the-moment. That will then be the time for you to start giving them as much independence as they're able to handle. And the psychological principle behind this course of action is people learn best by doing things themselves (8).

Sometimes infants will squall and cry for reasons you might not be able to understand initially, especially at night. This is the time for holding them and soothing whatever "beast" is roaming in their little psyches. And a time-honored way to do this is to rock them in your arms and sing to them. A rocking chair in the nursery is as important as a baby bed. So sing and rock your troubled infants' cares away.

Regarding music, introduce your children to good music as early as possible. It *does* soothe the savage beast and will instill in your children an appreciation of music, which can be a comfort and joy throughout life. It will also give them a sense of rhythm and harmony that will hold them in good stead later in life in areas where these things are important, such as athletics and dancing. There's also good evidence that music boosts intellectual development (9).

So don't worry about spoiling your infants. As they mature, gradually lead them into independent, responsible, need-fulfilling behavior. You do want them to leave your "nest" and strike out on their own someday, don't you?

CHAPTER 3

ABSTRACT CHILDREN

At his point, I'm going to introduce you to a concept that few people have ever heard of, but one you need to know about if you are going to raise children who are adaptable in an ever-changing world. That concept is *cognitive complexity* and arises out of the work of psychologist O. J. Harvey, Ph.D., (1).

Simply put, cognitive complexity is the degree and manner in which the neural pathways of the brain have been "programmed" through learning experiences. This learning and programming of our brains continues throughout our lives, of course, but it is most critical in our learning experiences as children. There is an old saying: "Give me the child 'til the age of six, and he's mine the rest of his life." Preschool and kindergarten programs are based on this premise, and most parents support these programs. An educational psychologist friend of mine once told me that half of all the programming-learning that we experience in life is done before the age of three! This indicates that what we parents do in teaching our children at this early stage is critical.

More specifically, Dr. Harvey and his colleagues defined this learning, calling the outcome "cognitive complexity," phrasing it in terms of *concreteness-abstractness*. To simplify his concept, imagine a line of one hundred people arrayed in front of you, from left to right. At the far left would be the most rigid, block-headed, non-changing person you know. (We know many people like that, don't we?) Dr. Harvey would call this person a *concrete* thinker. Now, as your eyes scan from left to right, these people become less concrete, more adaptable, and less rigid in their thinking—until you get to the farthest person on the right. Harvey would classify this person as a very *abstract* thinker, one who could see several solutions to a complex problem, who is willing to experiment and try new things.

Harvey has broken his *concreteness-abstractness* continuum down into four rough categories: System I, System II, System III, and System IV, with

System I being the most concrete and System IV the most abstract.

Here's the surprising part: Extensive research has shown that most people in America are concrete thinkers, there being about 70 percent of them in the general population. In four studies at two major universities, System I comprised 30 to 50 percent of the student population, while only 1 to 7 percent were System IV. The rest of the students were Systems II and III. The conclusion that we are forced to face is, even in our university system, there aren't many abstract thinkers (2)!

You may not think that a bad thing—but I do. So let me describe in detail what it means to be a concrete thinker, and then you can decide if that's what you want your children to become.

The following characteristics have been demonstrated in numerous studies to be correlated with System I, concrete personalities (3):

1) They have simpler thinking structures.

2) They have a greater tendency toward polarized, black-white thinking.

3) They are more status conscious.

4) They are more obedient to authority and less apt to raise questions about authoritative behavior.

5) They don't handle vague situations well.

6) They have more difficulty in changing their behavior when needed.

7) They tend to deal with complex problems the same way, repeatedly.

8) They want things to stay the same.

9) They have trouble seeing the forest for the trees, tending to get the means and the ends mixed up.

10) They're less sensitive to subtleties and nuances, thus are more susceptible to be sold a "bill of goods" by propagandists and charlatans.

11) They have less empathy for others.

12) They are low in task orientation, or getting the job done.

13) They have a greater tendency to form generalized impressions of others from highly incomplete information, thus are more likely to become prejudiced.

I might add that the more intelligent System I people are, the cleverer they are in maintaining their rigid thinking styles.

Conversely, abstract people have been found to be just the reverse on the above thirteen dimensions. Abstract thinkers tend to see things as various shades of grey, as opposed to black or white. They are not particularly status conscious. They tend to question authorities, recognizing that many authorities claim a certainty about things that do not exist. Authority that becomes dysfunctional or irrational girds them into opposition. They are comfortable in vague situations, ready to change course of action when needed. They tend to look for new solutions to old problems. They like change and welcome its challenges. They see the details that others miss. It's hard to sell them ideas unless they're based on facts. They have empathy for others but can be rather dispassionate if necessary to get the job done.

In my own personal counseling experience, concrete thinkers are more prone to develop mental illness than are the other System types. In thirty years as a mental health rehabilitation counselor, testing about a thousand mentally ill clients on these dimensions of *concreteness-abstractness*, I found only one System IV! All the rest were Systems I, II, and III—with System I in the majority by far. This illustrates that abstract people cope with the problems of the world better than most (4).

You may ask why this is so, but I can only give you a speculative opinion; further research is needed. First, life presents us all with problems, from birth and throughout our lives. And it's the big, traumatic incidences that impact us the most, especially those that repeat. When these bad things happen—and the more concrete our thinking processes—the more simplistic our reasoning is as to why all this is happening to us. And such a process leaves us little leeway to escape our own fears, doubts, and emotional turmoil that, when repeated over time, can lead to the formation of a distorted worldview—or mental/emotional illness. Thus, the obvious conclusion from all this is it's best to be relatively abstract, because abstract thinking better handles adaptation, diversity, and even survival itself!

The question then becomes how · abstract should people be? My answer is you don't have to worry about that because American society is relatively concrete, as is the rest of the world. The social learning that your children will get in school, church, and other activities will essentially be concrete in nature, and you will be in a constant struggle to promote abstractness within this larger concrete, societal-learning environment. To produce totally abstract children is not possible, nor is it desirable, because those children will have to live in a predominantly concrete world. So your goal should be to introduce your children to as much abstract-producing learning as possible, with the assurance that the larger society will temper it so that your children will fit in with the rest of the crowd.

In fact, it's erroneous to stamp absolute value judgments on people because of their degree of concreteness-abstractness. In this world, we really do need all types. For example, some jobs demand routine, repetitive thinking, for which concrete thinkers are better suited. However, some jobs demand flexible, out-of-the-box thinking and require abstract people. Of course, all jobs require us to use all types of thinking from time to time, but it is easier for abstract thinkers to merge into the more concrete mode of thinking than it is for concrete thinkers to become more abstract.

In raising my own children, I tried to make them more abstract than concrete, and shaped my child-rearing practices accordingly. However, the rest of their world had its influence also, so they turned out to be fairly abstract thinkers, with enough concreteness to deal effectively with the world around them.

But just what, you may ask, are these abstract-producing, child-rearing practices? Well, Dr. Harvey and his associates hypothesized that the following practices promote the development of the four System types:

SYSTEM I: These people are assumed to evolve from childhoods where the children are restricted in exploring their environment, especially that part concerned with society's values and the power inherent in various relationships. The children have very little exposure to diversity in social norms and are rewarded and punished according to what values the parents want to instill in the children. Basically, the parents have a narrow range of behaviors they reward, while having a much wider range they wish to discourage through punishment. The bad behaviors are usually those that are forbidden by God, Allah, the law, society, or simply, Mom and Dad's rules. This type of child rearing tends to produce children who greatly identify with a closed belief system, or what I call "It's my way or the highway!" syndrome. These children tend to become adults whose consciences are ruled by their versions of what they think the authority of their understanding wants them to do (5). It's probably safe to say that almost all of the Muslim terrorists who believe that they will be rewarded in Heaven for all the infidels they kill are extreme System I cases, as would be all the Ku Klux Klan members and Nazis who participate in lynchings and other horrific activities. The scary part of this is System I's are in the majority worldwide, across all religions and other ideological systems.

You can then see that religion and other non-religious belief systems, such as environmentalism, political persuasions, gun control attitudes, anti-abortion beliefs, and others, if pounded into the heads of our children sufficiently, and in the wrong manner, along with the wrong attitudes, can produce some iron-headed adults who will be most difficult to deal with in a rational, problem-solving manner.

It's my belief, and was my practice with my own children, to teach them to worship the God of our church, yet to teach them that God is a loving god, who has rules and expectations for us, but who also knows that we are not perfect and are going to make mistakes from time to time. And they should not expect that the answer to all life's problems will come from their religion.

There was a time when religion was viewed as the answer to most of our problems, but this is no longer the case. We now have other ways to solve many of life's problems, such as psychology, medicine, sociology, physics, politics, etc. We no longer live in the Stone Age.

Since there is often a large gap between certain religious beliefs and science, this issue had to be dealt with. I suggested to my clients that science is not a religion, but a method that humankind has developed to investigate the mysteries of our world and to solve many of our problems. However, science will often solve one problem, only to open the door to even more perplexing problems, such as birth control promoting increased sexual freedom or electricity consuming huge amounts of hydrocarbon fuels in its generation.

Science is the study of natural phenomenon, but science is not the end in itself. Rather, it is a process or method—and not a perfect method, either—that we use to study our universe. It is not to be viewed as the end-all system, but is simply the best method that we have yet devised, and until something better is developed, it will have to do.

When children are exposed to the principles of science and the family's religious system, they need to learn how to keep the proper perspective on both without becoming confused. Children who cannot integrate religion with science usually identify strongly with one and drop the other. And some simply drop both of them out of their lives, living a not-knowing, day-to- day existence.

The potential threat to religious fundamental-ists from science is they fear that, sooner or later, someone is going to use the process of science and discover something that goes against a basic tenet of their religion. And that would be anxiety provoking to say the least. One answer to this fear is if we assume science is God-given, then it is good, and whatever we discover with science *ought to be*. Thus we should move ahead with the resultant discoveries, make the appropriate adjustments, and deal with the consequences.

Abstract people can more easily do this. Parents who leave science out of their children's lives for fear of contamination of their basic religious beliefs are overreacting and doing them a disservice. If you look back over the history of science and the various religions, you will note that science marches on, no matter what. And, yes, it is sometimes tragic that the major religions move so slowly in their responses, but that is because our emotions and their traditions are not as flexible and fast moving as are our thinking processes. Science, being housed more in our rational, thinking mind, can move a faster pace than can religion, which dwells in the slower-changing, more emotional, mystical areas of our psyches.

Even so, the major religions have made adjustments in beliefs and practices when necessary. In fact, the scientific method evolved out of the conflict between Galileo's discoveries and the Roman Catholic Church. And we should not forget that one of the major functions of religion is to answer those questions that are beyond the realm of science: What happens to us after we die? Or does the human soul really exist? These are questions your children will need answers to someday.

The best exposition of this conflict between religion and science in recent years was the famous Scopes trial in Tennessee in 1927, when a high school teacher was tried and found guilty for teaching the theory of evolution in his classroom. This trial was later dramatized into a play and then made into an excellent movie in 1958, titled *Inherit the Wind*. If you haven't seen this movie, please do. It dramatizes this conflict between religion and science in an excellent manner.

SYSTEM II: System II results from deficient upbringing. Mainly, the parents are inconsistent—one time rewarding a certain behavior and the next time punishing it. Following the punishment, the parents may feel guilty about their capriciousness and overindulge their children to assuage these feelings of guilt. These child-rearing practices induce too much diversity in the developing child and tend to promote feelings of uncertainty, distrust of authority, and rejection of socially approved behavior. System II children are in constant rebellion, are strongly motivated to do it their way, and avoid dependency on God or other authorities in their lives (6). In my experience, the types of parents who tend to produce System II children are alcohol and drug addicted, absent, indifferent, emotionally dysfunctional, or overwhelmed with the responsibilities of parenthood—especially poor, single mothers. These latter parents practice what I call the "old woman in a shoe" syndrome whereby they use overly harsh child-rearing methods just to maintain order!.

In many ways, most of the System II behavior is an attempt by the child to say, "Hey, pay attention to me, and discipline me when I need it. I'm just a kid and I need you to teach me the ways of life!" Often, these children, who don't get what they need at home, will seek it from similar, rebellious friends, or gangs, who we know are not good teachers. They rarely get what they need from these "friends." The cases of unwed mothers, who have no males in the household, are especially tragic. Young boys need males in their lives to teach them how to become good men. Women can't teach boys some things that males need to know, so the children try to get it elsewhere—often with disastrous results.

SYSTEM III: System III consists of fairly abstract people and is believed to arise from child-rearing practices whereby the parents overprotect and overindulge their children. Then, one or both parents serve as a buffer between their children and the demands they face in society. This, in turn, prevents the growing children from freely exploring their physical and social world, forcing them to learn to get along by manipulating the parents (and later everyone else) to get what they need/ want (7). Restated, "If you don't give me enough freedom to figure out a large part of life on my own, then I'll just manipulate you to get what I need." System III children usually develop excellent skills at getting other people to do things for them. They tend to get into jobs dealing with people, such as counselors, social workers, salespeople, and the like.

SYSTEM IV: System IV children are developed when their parents and others in their lives give them the freedom to explore all aspects of their environment, consistent with safety, health, and community responsibilities. They have stability in their childhoods and are exposed to a variety of people and ways of approaching life's situations. They are treated as individuals in their own right, and their demands and reasons are given due consideration—though not always granted. They are not overindulged or pampered. Discipline is usually administered by negative behavior being followed by natural or parentally established consequences: "If you don't eat your squash, then you'll get nothing more to eat until the next meal." (8)

A key point here is that the parents do not try to dominate or shape the children into a certain mold, but try to lead the children to approach the world with a curious, searching, problem-solving orientation. The parents are trying to get the children to discover their talents and abilities and develop them according to their own interests. These children are encouraged to seek their own responses to life, with the parents as observers and guides, and their solutions are treated with respect. They are rewarded for *trying* as much as *succeeding*. The mantra around their household would be, "It's not whether you win or lose it's how you play the game!"

Of course, it's easy to see that, for children like this, information has high value to them, causing them to become autonomous, with appropriate dependence on others. The answers they develop to life's problems tend to be *relativistic*. System I people, who want *the* correct answer, are driven crazy by these folks. We might also say that System IV children tend to become somewhat scientific in their approach to life.

Now that you have an understanding of the System types, what should you parents do? We certainly don't want a brood of rebellious System II people who are always fighting the "System," either burning their bras or the flag, angry at all our law enforcement officers, hating the military establishment and corporate CEOs, and disgusted with our government officials and other authority figures, do we?

But we also don't want them to become bleeding hearts, social welfarists, or those who believe all of our society's disadvantaged have no free will of their own and are total victims of the rest of us, and by damn, they're going to save all those poor souls by manipulating the system to get those poor people what is rightfully due them.

And we don't want our children to become blind followers of *all* authority, be it God as interpreted by others, governmental officials, the media, crackpot friends and relatives, and loony public figures.

Of course not. Not the readers of this book, anyway. We want our children to grow into adults who are most like System IV, but who also have some of the desirable characteristics of the other Systems on our continuum. We want our children to be reasonable, loving, assertive, social, adventurous, respectful, curious, and tolerant.

The rest of this book is designed to help you develop such children.

CHAPTER 4

THINKING SKILLS

Psychologists break down the basic processes that go on in the human brain to *thinking* and *feeling*. The terms they use are *cognitive* and *affective*, respectively. In this chapter, we are considering the *thinking* aspect of your children (1).

We need not look far in today's society to see that clear, objective, rational, flexible, thinking skills seem to be in short supply these days. Listening to "experts" on talk shows debate the issues of the day, we get the definite impression that a lot of thinking skills are being diverted to support various personal opinions, and these are most often only loosely connected to the facts or reality. What is sad is that these bogus opinions often come from some very astute and educated people.

This distressing situation shows that clear thinking should be well grounded in reality and the facts. But reality and the facts are often hard to determine. There doesn't seem to be enough scientific, rational thinking going on these days.

Without getting too technical, children need to learn how to think scientifically. They need to learn how to observe the world around them accurately, develop sensible ideas about what they see, develop the ability to gather further needed information, and then come up with solutions to their problems.

How, you may ask, do parents go about instilling all this in children? The short answer is you're already doing most of it when you interact with your children. By speaking to your children, you are teaching them your language, and language skills are the basis for all that follows. Taking them to the zoo teaches them about animals. Reading to your children introduces them to a whole world of various ideas and things. In short, every new thing in which developing children engage is stretching their brains to ever-increasing new limits. And, by the way, don't worry about overtaxing your children's mental limits, because for all practical purposes, there are no limits! For instance, it has been estimated by neurologists that the human brain has about one hundred billion neurons, which are the brain cells that store the information we learn. And the possible number of ways that this mass of neurons can interconnect with one another to form new learning pathways *exceeds the total number of atoms in the known universe* (2)!

Astounded? You should be! But you should also be happy, because your children have "computers" in their heads that have unlimited RAM, to use a computer-capacity term! This means that they have enough capacity for you to teach them all they'll ever need.

So, how do you get your children onto the path of scientific thinking? And just what does this mean? Will my child become a sort of scientific egghead? And, hey, you may not want a nerd for a child. After all, they make funny movies about nerds!

Relax. "Nerdism" does not develop out of scientific, problem-solving thinking. Was Colombo a nerd? Or Perry Mason? How about our business leaders or professional people, be they white or blue collar? Of course, some are nerds—but most aren't, because nerdism is more a personality quirk than anything else. All scientific-type minds do is promote clear, rational, critical, problem-solving thinking.

I don't know how you see it, but good problem solvers seem to be becoming increasingly rare these days. Have you had an automobile problem lately that no one seems to be able to fix on the first or second attempt? The deficiency is not because of a lack of tools or equipment, but is the inability to think as trained mechanics should, in a critical, problem-solving manner. When I was in the Air Force, I maintained and repaired some very complex weapons systems on all-weather fighter interceptors. This was in the late 1950s and the aircraft used the electronic technology of the day, which was much less dependable than what we have today. The electronic systems needed constant care and attention, because they were constantly breaking down. Some of the technicians were quite proficient in maintaining the equipment properly, but about a third of the technicians caused more problems than they resolved. This was despite the fact that everyone had the same level of training. The point here is, very often, despite excellent training, some people can't utilize that training properly to get the job done. And my experience suggests that it is an inability to do critical, rational, problem-solving thinking.

We should recognize that there are degrees of differences from one child to the next in their capacity to learn scientific-type thinking, with the more intelligent children being able to deal with more complex problems. However, life is not rocket science, so all children can learn this process sufficiently to get along in the world. And it takes two sets of people, in general, to teach children these skills: parents and teachers, whoever those teachers might be. And the earlier the process begins the more effect it has. In fact, it's my contention that most of this teaching work has to be done before puberty, before the hormones kick in! At puberty, parents and teachers lose a lot of control to children's peer groups. And believe me, teenage peers will not teach critical thinking skills to your children. At this point, hormones and peer associations rule the day!

Let's look at the influence of parents and teachers first. It begins at home, goes into preschool and kindergarten, then the first grade in school. Mathematics and reading, primarily, begin the structuring of the brain in ways we are seeking. The order to numbers, words, and symbols is begun. Relationships to numbers and words are developed. Children start playing word and number games. They see what other people are doing in this regard. They like riddles and rhymes and solving puzzles. They are very good at memorizing things. As they progress in school their education gets more complex. By high school they should have learned how to add, subtract, multiply, divide, do percentages and fractions, and write a decent letter. They are now getting ready to take courses such as algebra, geometry, trigonometry, solid geometry, analytic geometry, and perhaps, calculus. Biology, chemistry, physics, history, literature, and English composition round out a good basic education.

"But wait," some of you may say, "aren't these the courses that college-bound kids in technical fields take? All kids don't need to take these courses, do they?"

My answer is all children who are able should take as many of these basic academic courses as they can. The learning of mathematics, for instance, structures and programs the brain in ways that facilitates the ability to do the type of mental operations critical to rational, scientific thinking. They learn to do essential numerical calculations, to picture lines, angles, and forms-in-space in their mind's eye. And no matter what occupation one eventually enters, mathematics will be a part of that job. Artists, architects, and engineers especially need to know about the world of lines, curves, and angles. Whether it's the baseball outfielder tracking a fly ball, the hunter leading the dove on the fly with his shotgun, the basketball player arcing a jump shot, or the golfer calculating the distance and trajectory of his shot to the green, all need to have angles, arcs, and distances as a part of their repertoire of behavior to effectively perform.

The mother shopping in the grocery store, keeping a rough running total of her purchases before checkout so she won't overspend, needs to know how to add in her head or use a handheld calculator—or have lots of money! The home-owner, cutting risers for some new steps, needs to know how to do the intricate geometry on a carpenter's square and how to measure accurately. Anyone working on the engine of an automobile needs to know how to measure in thousands of an inch with a micrometer and how to convert inches into centimeters and millimeters. There are countless ways that mathematics is interwoven into our lives, so we don't need to belabor the point.

But many of you will say that you don't do such intricate work, that you simply pay an expert or professional to do it for you. And that's fine, but please remember that the world we now live in is changing at an accelerating pace, and not all for the good. Social systems are now more lax, so you are more at the mercy of crooks, charlatans, and incompetents and they will take advantage of you if you can't think in certain critical ways. A friend of mine was quoted a price on re-roofing his house, based on him having three thousand square feet of roof. Now, my friend was not mathematically minded, having taken as little math in his school years as he could get by with, and he was ready to pay the roofer what he'd asked. But when I looked at the house, it just didn't "look" like three thousand square feet. So, using some simple math and basic trigonometry skills, I calculated his actual square footage and saw that it was only a bit over two thousand square feet! Thus the contractor's estimate of the cost was more than a third higher than it should have been. Later, in talking with this contractor—the so-called roofing expert—it became clear that he had no more math skills than did my friend; he wasn't a crook, just incompetent in this area. Thus, my math skills saved my friend $1,000.

The main point here is that mathematics structures your brain to operate in ways that are very useful in working on the problems life presents to you. Another way to put it is what an old soldier friend of mine said: "You know, Joe, when you're in mortal combat, you can't have too many bullets in your gun!" That goes for your children's brains as well! And life is sometimes like mortal combat!

Next, let's look at reading and writing skills. There was a time in America when most children graduating from high school could read almost any text you put in front of them, and they'd at least have a rough idea of what the author was saying. And these kids could write a letter to Mom and she'd know what they were saying to her. This is not necessarily so anymore.

As one who has evaluated the writing and reading skills of thousands of people over the past thirty years as a vocational rehabilitation counselor, I can state categorically that very few high school—or college graduates—can write a sound, error-free business letter. Reading and writing skills seem to have been given over to TV watching and computer usage, which, in turn, has led to the development of people who can "talk the game but can't play it."

A colleague of mine, a vocational evaluator, came to me one day, very puzzled and perplexed. She said, "Joe, you're not going to believe this, but I just got two new clients for vocational evaluation and testing, but both of them have reading and math skills at the third and fourth grade levels!"

"What's so unusual about that?" I asked, knowing that we had many clients who didn't go far in school.

"But, Joe, these two clients both have master's degrees in education and were high school teachers, one in Mississippi and one in Alabama!"

Well, I about fell out of my chair. I didn't see how such a thing could be possible, but she showed me their test scores—which were administered twice, in case there was a mistake. But there was no doubt—these two people were incompetent as teachers, and this may have played a part in them winding up as mental patients.

She went on, "When I presented this data to them, they were defiant and unbelieving, accusing me of racism and threatening to call our supervisor. I had told them that our agency could not support them in any sophisticated job training until they got their reading and math skills up to the high school level."

She went on to describe these two people: a man and a woman who were attractive and sophisticated looking, who could speak very well, but who had been poorly educated by school systems that were more concerned about appearances, social promotions, and other issues than they were about properly educating their students (3).

This was an extreme case, of course, but don't fool yourself into thinking that it's not a fairly common scenario—because it is.

Looking at language skills, why are reading and writing so important? Because humans are language animals. We are what we are because of our ability with language. When we think, we think in streams of sentences that are language, without which we couldn't think. Oh, I suppose we could think like a dog or a cat, using images of things we have seen, but I'm sure we want our children to be smarter than Fido!

People vary in language ability, as they do in math, but I've proven to myself, through my many clients over the years, that most of this variance is due to poor education, reading deficiencies, lack of interest, poor parental examples, too much TV, etc. The point is, to read and write effectively, one must do a lot of it while growing up, encouraged and nurtured by the parents and school.

Many of my teacher friends say that most of the problems they have with their students begin at home, with the main problem being that the children never see their parents read! Of course, if children never see Mom or Dad read, why should they? Conversely, the kids who do read seem to come from those families where they are read to at an early age, have reading materials available, are limited in TV watching and computer game playing, and whose parents read a variety of materials. Monkeys see, monkeys do!

I need to make a critical point here: For those parents who have a problem with authority, you should not teach that disrespect to your children and lay it in the teachers' laps. Teachers are your friends. Most are trying to help you and your children. The majority of your local taxes go into their salaries. Support them. Do not put them in the position where it's you versus them. If your children have an appropriate amount of homework, be thankful and assume that your child's teacher believes that she can handle it, or it wouldn't have been assigned. If your children get lazy with their schoolwork and get bad grades, get on the side of the teacher and let your precious darlings know that you and the teacher are a team and that you expect your children to do whatever the teacher assigns.

A good strategy is for the parents to visit with the teachers on the days when the PTA sets up parental visits. This is usually an open house-type affair at the school, with the parents, teachers, and students all in the school building together. Questions can be asked, comments made, all with the goal that you, as the parents, are there to support the system in giving your child a good education. Tell the teachers that you expect your children to perform to the limits of their abilities and any help they need from you will be forthcoming. Let your children hear you say these things to the teachers, because that will bond all of you into an efficient learning unit.

Do not—ever—paint your children's teachers and the school system as some sort of problem in your children's minds. Do not say negative things about the school in front of the children. And the younger the children, the more critical this point is. Young children do not yet have the capacity to evaluate and sort out many of the teaching/ school problems that inevitably arise from time to time. When a problem arises that needs attention, schedule an appointment with the teacher or other appropriate staff member to discuss the situation. There is almost no situation that cannot be handled this way. Further, it is important that you never make the teacher feel that he or she is the problem—even if he or she is—because if you do, your children will be the losers.

If you approach the school system with this attitude and participate in PTA and other parental school activities, you will see a curious thing happen: Your children will tend to become "favored students" and will get that little extra "something" from their teachers in the way of assistance and considerations, which will make the whole learning experience a pleasure to all.

If you stop and think about it, teachers, to whom we trust our precious children six to eight hours every day, are often underpaid relative to other professions and deserve our utmost respect and support. It is my contention that the most influential people your children will meet in their entire lives will be their parents and teachers. The others don't even come close. And the younger the children, the more important they are.

Once upon a time, I was invited to a big university fundraiser that was sponsored by my national church body. Everyone was saying how wonderful this university was, how well it was shaping the young men and women who were students there. While there were no "animal house" activities going on at this college, my interaction with the students who had graduated there showed them to be no better or worse than the average, run-of-the-mill college graduates.

Then I noted that the school had only nine hundred or so students, but it cost millions of dollars to run the place. The dollars-to-benefit ratio didn't look too good, so I mentioned this to a group of ardent supporters of this university:

"You know, folks, all of the educational research—which I am sure you are familiar with [they weren't, of course]— shows that, from an educational point of view, if you want to influence young people's minds in the way our church would like, you need to do it at as early an age as possible. This will maximize the type of learning we would want to instill in them. In fact, if you haven't gotten to them by college, it's essentially too late. After a bit of study, I've noticed that our church has colleges and seminaries all over the country, but we have very few elementary or high schools. Now, if I understand the notion of church-supported schools, it is that we church members want our children to be educated in a climate that teaches them the ways of our world in a Christian context. What I'm saying is the best time to do that is in elementary school. So what do you say if we look at the idea of starting some church-supported elementary schools in our city and put some of this money that we're raising where it'll do the most good?"

As you might imagine, my discourse went over like a screen door in a submarine. Hardly anyone would speak to me thereafter, and I have not been asked to contribute to that university since.

The point of all this is to emphasize to you, the parents, that the earlier you and the school system can begin to influence your children, the better.

CHAPTER 5

EMOTIONAL SKILLS

A psychiatrist who I once met at a counselor training conference said that the human emotional world can be boiled down to *mad*, *glad*, *sad*, and *afraid*. He was talking about *anger*, *happiness*, *depression*, and *fear*. These are the basic feelings that all humans deal with in life, and if they handle them well, they will be successful (1).

You will note that there are three "bad" feelings (mad, sad, and afraid) and only a single "good" one (happiness). Realizing this is somewhat an oversimplification of the human emotional system, the psychiatrist said the academics and researchers may want to expand this list into a more complex "feeling system," but the fact remains that most of us go about our lives seeking happiness, and we are quite well satisfied if we can keep anger, depression, and fear under some sort of reasonable control.

Thus, the parents' goal should be to develop a sense of well-being, or happiness, in their children and teach their children how to manage and control anger, sadness, and fear. These negative emotions continually arise in our lives, but in fact, they are really not negative at all, but are our friends, as we shall see later. The trick is to teach your children how to manage them and make them work *for* them—which, of course, will then make your children happy. More about that later.

Most parents become aware of the emotional world of their children when they enter the time often called the "terrible twos." This is around the age of two years old, when the children's physical and mental development has progressed to the point that they can move around freely, engage in limited conversation, and play. Having learned a lot about this world, they are generally charming little people—most of the time (2)!

But then comes the day when you ask them to do something that they don't want to do. At this point, they may put their hands on their hips, look defiantly at you, and give you a loud, defiant "No!"

At this stage of their lives, they have begun to develop an ego and awareness of the world, and have learned that they are relatively free little human beings and can choose to obey or not. At this point, you, the parents, are now at "war" with your children.

The first rule is to stay calm and do not get angry. In fact, be thankful that you have children with a little spunk. You now know this is the beginning of their learning about authority and how to deal with it. And dealing appropriately with authority in this world is one of the most important skills they'll ever acquire, because everyone will have bosses in their lives, and dealing with them is important.

Before you react to their "No!" you need to know what you're going to do and why. Parents who don't handle this early conflict well wind up angry or depressed about it and are at risk of being stuck with children who are chronically defiant, selfish, self-centered, and hard to live with (3).

It really is a battle that the parents must win—without destroying the children's egos and sense of self-worth. The thing *not* to do on a regular basis is using force to make children comply. All this will do is develop children who are always at war with you, because they *must*—and should—defend their developing egos against all attackers, including parents! Some parents are successful using force and excessive punishment in the children's early years, only to experience increasing rebellion and alienation during the teen years.

If your children happen to be passive, those who obey your every command, then you'll likely get the opposite effect: Those who are shy, submissive, and probably depressed later on as adults. Or you might get a combination: Those who seem to comply on the surface, but sneak around your back and do whatever they please when you're not looking.

When your children start saying no to your directives and you perceive your children are ready to understand simple logic, take them aside, sit them down, look them straight in the eye with a look of love (not anger), and say something like this:

"Now, Billy, I know you don't want to do what I just asked you to, but it's very important that you do what I say, because I'm your father (or mother). And I'm trying to teach you those things that you need to know about so you'll grow up and do well and be happy, like Mommy and Daddy. People can't always do whatever they want to. Even I have to obey rules, like stopping at red lights in the car, taking out the garbage so the house won't stink, doing what my boss tells me so I can earn money to buy food so we all can eat. When we play games, we all have to follow the rules, or the games don't work right. You know what happens when you play games with other boys and girls and they don't follow the rules, don't you?"

(Wait for an answer.)

"Not much fun, is it? Well, I'm trying to teach you the rules of this family, and it's important for all of us to be fair and play by the rules. So, I'll make a deal with you. The next time I ask you to do something and you don't want to do it, I want you to say, 'Daddy, I don't want to do that, and here's the reason why.' Then I want you to tell me why. Then we'll talk about it, like we're doing now. And if you give me a good enough reason, I might not make you do it. Is that a deal?"

(Again, wait for an answer.)

Usually, they'll agree, but if they don't, go through the whole scenario again. You might want to vary the examples and the language to better fit their particular level of understanding. But do not adjourn this session without an agreement. When you have an agreement, then do something to reward your children, which will solidify your relationship and role as parents. You may have to repeat this process several times until your children "get it," but stick to your resolve.

A process like this directs the education of children to becoming more *rational* people, as opposed to being *emotional* people. The above conversation may be too much for some children at age two, but something like this should take place sooner or later to establish the parents' authority and control. If it is done in a calm, rational manner similar to this, it will give the children the message that their parents can be talked to and will listen—but first they have to do some preliminary thinking and come up with some good reasons. And it makes them struggle with their emotions and gain control over them.

There will be times, of course, when you cannot do all this. For example, when an incident occurs in a public place, then you have to do whatever is reasonable to maintain control and authority, and do the talking later. A little slap on the fanny is sometimes necessary to get children's attention. Other times, you might have to pick up children while they're kicking and screaming about not getting their way and physically remove them from the scene. Light spanking is okay and is parents' only recourse at times. Remember, it is important that the children know that the parents are in ultimate control. In the long run, this knowledge gives the children a sense of comfort and stability. You can imagine the anxiety that would be induced in children if they always won these battles over their parents, because deep down they know that they don't know much, but these stupid parents of theirs keep caving in to them as if they did know! What an uncertain world that is!

Now, let's get back to the basic negative emotions of anger, sadness, and fear and what to do about them. After discussing these, we will then deal with happiness, and you'll see how they all fit together.

A primary point I want to make about emotions is they never lie to you! Is that statement astounding to you? Consider the following point of view and I'm sure you'll agree, mainly because few people ever think of negative feelings this way. And a corollary to this is that your emotions—especially the negative ones—are the best friends you'll ever have!

Take anger. Everyone has been angry. Think back to the last time you were angry and you will find that there was probably a good reason for your anger. Perhaps you were in a traffic situation and someone cut you off, almost causing a collision. Immediately, you got angry, and justifiably so, because the person put you at risk. Now, are you going to say you shouldn't get angry in such a situation? I don't think so. The anger has now made you hyper alert, your adrenaline's flowing, and you're now more quickly responsive to handle this dangerous situation. The other driver is obviously in violation of the rules of the road, in that he or she didn't give you a proper signal, so your anger in this situation is justifiable.

The next question is what to do about it. In this situation, you might use your anger to honk your horn to let the other driver know that he or she put you at risk and you don't appreciate it. On the other hand, you could just "swallow" the anger and do nothing, but that's not good for one's mental health, especially if it becomes a habit. Further, action on the road would probably be inappropriate since it might lead to a "road rage" incident, causing an even bigger problem. So the next step should be to calm yourself down by recognizing that the world's full of stupid drivers and you will continue to be alert to their misdeeds.

The trick with anger is to *listen* to it, see what causes it, deal with it in the most rational, problem-solving manner possible, and then move on. Where most people get stuck is to get angry, overreact and get aggressive, or do nothing about it, stew over it until it makes them sick, complain about it to anyone who will listen over and over, and never deal with the primary cause. We need to practice using our anger constructively, dealing with it, and teaching this process to our children. In the chapter on "Assertiveness Training" we will be dealing with the specifics of how to do this and how to teach your children to be appropriately assertive.

Next, there are a lot of theories about the causes of depression or sadness. Clinical depression is beyond sadness, of course, but it is sufficient to know that depression can arise from several sources: a chemical imbalance in the brain, brutal life experiences, significant life losses, suppressed anger, chronic negative thinking about one's self, and combinations of these (4). We don't need to go into all this in detail, but it is important for you to know that there are child-rearing contributors to the above causes of sadness. We will deal with these causes so that you can understand them and raise your children so they can manage their lives in ways to minimize their sadness episodes.

The kind of depression that comes from a chemical imbalance, of which chronic alcohol and drug abuse can be a cause, is best handled by the afflicted person seeking professional help. Any parents who suffer from this type of depression should seek help and get themselves straightened out so as to lessen the chance of being inappropriate role models to their children. If you go around all day sad, blue, and depressed, you are teaching your children, by example, that the way to handle life's problems is to be depressed like Mommy or Daddy. Then the rest of the family has to make a maladaptive adjustment to "work around" the sick person's behavior.

I once had an elderly lady client who was taught in childhood to never show her anger because it wasn't ladylike. As an adult, she didn't know how to express her anger, so in response to a very bad marriage, she got depressed and went to her bed—and remained there for years, feigning some mysterious illness! Of course, the rest of the family had to spend a disproportionate amount of their time tending to their "sick" mother. Finally, the father got fed up and left all of them. The mother then miraculously recovered, got out of bed, and went about her life. Her two children, observing and participating in this, grew up to be depressed adults.

One of the main reasons why many inappropriate behaviors are perpetuated in families is that when parents live out lives of dysfunction, with the children observing all this and thinking it's normal behavior, they are then very prone to copying them, becoming dysfunctional themselves. Therefore, for those of you chronically depressed parents, no matter what the cause, you need to get professional help and set a different example for your kids. Otherwise, you may produce another generation of children with the same problems.

We do want our children to be better than us, don't we?

If you have the type of depression arising from negative childhood experiences, you need to develop an understanding of this, perhaps through professional help, reflection, or spiritual insight, and try to develop a more optimistic way of looking at life. This is not easy to do, but you really can't afford not to do it. You must develop the attitude of learning from your past experiences by reflecting on them and seeing what you could have done differently. From this process you can develop better responses for similar events in the future, thus teaching your children how to do the same.

Closely correlated with negative life-experience problems is the threat that significant *life losses* impose on us, such as the death of a loved one, losing a job, divorce, or the advent of a significantly disabling condition. But please recognize that what is a significant loss to you may not be the same to someone else. Usually, when one person doesn't feel devastated by a particular loss, and another does, the difference is attributable to one's attitude about the loss. In fact, one's devastating divorce may be another's newfound freedom—the difference being in their attitudes.

Regarding life losses, there are two basic ways to cope with them. The first and most efficient is to utilize those social institutions in our society that have already been developed to handle such situations. For example, funerals help the bereaved deal with death. (Or did you think funerals were for dead people?) Friends comfort us during this time of pain; the pastor conducts a formalized service and consoles us; friends offer us condolences, food, and other support; bosses give us time off from work; and relatives support each other. If you have lost a spouse to alcohol or drug abuse, there are Alanon and Alateen groups and meetings for spouses and children to learn how to cope, to not feel guilty, and to move on with their lives. For people who suffer other loses, there are other support groups for just about any loss imaginable. But you've got to use these resources and show your children how to use them by taking them with you when appropriate and explaining the process to them.

When my daughter was about six years old, just such a situation came up. A friend of mine's father died somewhat unexpectedly. My wife and I agreed that this was the time to teach our daughter about death and how to handle it. So I took my daughter out of school on the day of the funeral, because I knew that what she'd learn at the funeral would far surpass anything she could learn in that one day in the classroom. At the funeral, we went to the church, listened to the preacher, watched the family members weep, went to the graveside service, and stayed until the last shovel of dirt was thrown on the grave. My daughter observed all this intently, even felt a little sad, although she'd never met my friend's father. But she saw my friend's sadness and watched him and the other family members grieve. And she saw all the support around him and learned that the survivors of the death of a loved one could still go on with life. Thus, she got a sense of survival and security that day that serves her well today. And my friend said in later years that he remembered everything that went on that day, even down to the color and type of my daughter's dress, and that it helped him enormously that we were there. Needless to say, whenever we have needed anything of him, he has always been there for us.

The point of all this is that society has developed many ways to cope with losses in life. It is incumbent upon you to use these systems and introduce them to your children. Also, follow up your participation with an explanation to your children about what occurred and what it can mean to them. You don't have to get elaborate. Keep it simple.

The second way to cope with life's losses is to help your children develop the ability to put a positive spin on these losses, and to repeat this process enough so that it becomes a habit. Some examples are as follows:

1) After a death, use your religious beliefs to show your children that the departed one is now free of earthly pain, suffering, and struggle and is now in a better afterlife.

2) The children who strike out in a Little League game are way ahead in the game if they can say to themselves on the way back to the dugout, "He struck me out this time, but the best ballplayers in the world fail two out of three times, so I'll get that hit next time!"

3) The guy who asks a girl for a date and gets turned down needs to think, "I don't know why she turned me down, but it's her loss because I'm a pretty good guy, so I'll ask someone else—there are plenty of fish in the sea."

What we're talking about here is teaching your children consistent positive thinking—especially in the face of adversity. This stimulates a pattern of continual striving and not giving up. Children who develop this habit of thinking rarely get seriously depressed as adults, because this way of thinking is the antithesis of depression: You can't think positively and be depressed at the same time. (5)

A famous psychiatrist, Viktor Frankl, illustrates this point with the way he conducted his life after World War II. In many ways Frankl suffered as much as the legendary Job in the Bible. Frankl was a physician and a Jew in Nazi Germany. The Nazis imprisoned and killed the members of his family, but spared him because he was a doctor and was useful to them in that capacity. He saw his friends and colleagues die in the gas chambers, leading him to initially wonder as to the purpose of life if humankind was this evil and destructive. Later, he noticed that many of his condemned friends went into the gas chambers with their heads held high, and he ultimately came to the conclusion that, even with the Nazi's power, there was still one thing they couldn't take away: *the freedom to control one's own attitude under terrible circumstances!* They maintained a transcendental attitude based on all the positive beliefs they held. These condemned people became martyrs for all they held dear in life and no one had the power to take that away.

Frankl was subsequently inspired by these people to resist and survive, so he could later communicate to the world what he had learned about suffering. His attitude toward his and other's suffering enabled him to endure some of the most horrific events in human history. After the war he wrote books about his experiences, gave lectures around the world, and developed a type of psychotherapy that is still being practiced. His life, and his response to adversity, is an inspiration to all.

Another way to cope with depression or loss is to engage in strenuous physical activity on a regular basis. Numerous clinical studies have shown that regular aerobic and muscular exercise is a better antidepressant than are the major tranquilizer drugs! Physical activity stimulates the production of endorphins in the brain, which gives one a sense of well-being. And, of course, when you're feeling well, you can't be depressed (6).

So get your children moving physically at an early age—and keep them moving! Encourage them to participate in sports, to walk and run, to throw and hit balls. You won't have to work very hard here because most kids want to do these things. You just need to watch, demonstrate, and supervise so they'll do them appropriately. My wife and I required our children to play at least one organized team sport throughout their childhood years, right on through high school. They accepted this easily and did quite well. They had fun and developed habits that still keep them in superb physical shape as adults. And they learned some valuable lessons on how to get along with others in those situations where they were competing vigorously with and against others. These were valuable lessons.

Finally, let's look at negative thinking, or what my friends in Alcoholics Anonymous call "stinking thinking." Negative, self-deprecating thinking is the biggest cause of depression, in my opinion. I'm talking about those patterns of thought that run through our heads on a continual basis: "I can't do that!" "If I try, I'll fail." "Every time I do that I screw things up." "As hard as I try, I can never please him." "I'm too short for the basketball team."

You get the picture here. And it doesn't take much imagination to see that if folks develop this type of thinking to the point that it becomes chronic, then they're not going to attempt many challenges in life. As a result, will not live up to their potential as adults, because they'll never try many things in the first place. And those things they do strive for will likely get only halfhearted attempts, usually leading to expected failure.

Now, some children are born shy and insecure, and if not intervened upon by their parents, they are likely to stay that way and be prone to chronic negative thinking—especially about themselves. Other children are born positive thinkers, and the parents' job here will be to "rein" them in and keep them closely tied to what's real and appropriate. The great majority of children are somewhere between these extremes. Your task is to determine which type your children are and develop your child-rearing strategies accordingly. And believe me, you can have all three types in one family—as anyone from a big family can testify. Parents who were "only children," or who have only one or two children, might not realize this due to limited experience. Their perspective is usually to believe that the way things were with them is the way things will be with all children. When the parents' perspective is limited in this regard, and those little children sitting in front of them don't behave the way Mommy or Daddy did when they were children, confusion can set in. It may well be that there are genetically determined personality differences with which they find themselves quite unfamiliar.

So whatever type of children you were blessed with, it's important that you tailor your child-rearing practices to those that teach positive thinking. You do this by praising and rewarding good behavior. Within reason, never tell children that they're not able to do something. Let them try to find out for themselves. Encourage your children to try things they might initially be afraid of, but be there to console and give constructive feedback if they fail. The idea is it is better to have tried and failed than never to have tried at all. "Brand" that thought into their brains at an early age. Tell them that the best baseball hitters of all time succeeded only thirty-seven percent of the time. Tell them that one of the best golfers of all time said that, in a round of golf, only one or two shots out of seventy or so worked out exactly as planned—the rest were near misses. Tell them that the average millionaire in America failed nine times before finally making it and that most people quit after one or two tries. Tell them that professionals working with alcoholics in trying to help them get clean and sober, straighten out their lives, and go back to work fail three out of four times (7). Tell them that when all children are learning to walk, they fall down hundreds of times before they get it right—but they don't quit. If fact, failure only makes them try harder—and that's what you expect of them.

Finally, along with this line of thinking, I want to draw upon my experience of working in the electromechanical field and give you a concept with which all engineers are familiar but few have ever thought of in terms of raising children. I call it the "governor principle."

In the electromechanical world, there is a device called a "governor." The purpose of one type of governor is to regulate the speed of an engine. In this case, it's a device that receives mechanical information from the revolving engine as to how fast it's turning. The governor has been pre-set to keep the engine running at a constant speed, because without the governor the engine will go faster and faster, until it flies apart, destroying itself. The governor works by slowing the engine down when it goes too fast, and letting it speed up when it is too slow. The central point here is *the only information the governor constantly gets is error information*. It never gets correct information—only what's wrong! But with this constant feedback of what's going wrong all the time, it is able to make the necessary changes to keep the speed of the engine near the speed that has been predetermined.

You should teach your children that life consists of many more mistakes and errors than it does of things that are "right on the money." Errors are the majority of reality. Errors, therefore, have to be our friends. They tell us when things go wrong; thus, we can do something to correct them. Where we make our mistakes is when we don't accept this concept, expecting perfection instead. So get used to this concept, learn to use it, and teach it to your children. And please note that physical pains are feedback that something is wrong with your body, so please note and go to the doctor when appropriate.

Turning to fear, we see an emotion that arises when your children think something bad or terrible is going to happen. They may have done something bad and think they will be punished if they are caught. If the punishment quickly follows the misdeed, it will usually inhibit similar behavior in the future. If the bad behavior is regularly punished, then children will build up a reservoir of fear in their minds about what will happen in the future following such behavior, and that will usually inhibit them from doing the misdeed. As children grow older, parental threats will usually be enough to instill fear and prevent bad behavior. Eventually, the fear will morph over into guilt, and guilt is usually a very powerful preventer of misdeeds.

The problem with fear is it can spread and generalize to things that shouldn't be feared, and this usually comes about because children are not taught to be specific and detailed. Probably the biggest fear in America is that of snakes, to look at a concrete example. Nonpoisonous snakes are among the most harmless creatures around, and they cannot hurt your children as severely as can a dog or cat. In America, there are only four types of poisonous snakes: rattlesnakes, copperheads, water moccasins, and coral snakes. But because we adults are too fearfully ignorant or lazy to teach our children how to distinguish these poisonous types from the hundreds of others, we conveniently lump them all together and teach them to be fearful of all. Once children are afraid of all snakes, the fear usually generalizes to all "creepy-crawly" things. So if you want your children to be unafraid of snakes (or anything else, for that matter), expose them to some harmless ones at an early age. Let them hold the snakes and play with them. They will learn that they won't hurt them. Then teach them about the ones that are dangerous so they can discriminate and be careful. This process works with all potential objects of fear.

Fear of *failure* deserves some mention here. But as we have already noticed, failure happens more than success. To handle this, encourage and support your children to try and try again at whatever they're attempting, supporting them when they fail and urging them to go on. Then, when they finally succeed, reward them vigorously with praise and encouragement, pointing out that the success came only after much effort. Do this process over and over again, and soon, you'll have children who will never quit!

This principle is universal and illustrates a central principle in psychology: The way to increase a behavior is to reward your children frequently when they first succeed, then gradually reward only intermittently. Rewarding children all the time may eventually cause them to lose interest because of boredom, getting too much of a good thing, or looking for more variety. So reward success a lot at first, then only once in a while (8).

We have now dealt with anger, fear, and depression. We'll go even further into anger in Chapter 8. Now let's look at *glad*, or happiness.

Happiness, and the pursuit of it, is so critical that our nation's Founding Fathers featured it as a primary reason behind the Declaration of Independence. The pursuit of happiness might even be called humankind's primary pastime. However, happiness is somewhat hard to define. We all know "happiness" when we see it in others or experience it ourselves, but it's hard to put into words and explain to others because it's such a subjective feeling. But we must define it sufficiently to understand it so we can teach it to our children!

Happiness is a pleasant feeling, or state-of-being, that comes over us when we're getting those things out of life that we want and need. A good job, plenty of money, a good spouse, enough leisure time, vacations, holidays, meaningful things to do, hitting a home run, scoring the winning touchdown, a new car, graduation day—all are events or things that tend to make us happy in our lives. The problem arises when we can't secure them. It should be obvious by now that if we don't manage our emotions of mad, sad, and afraid, we are not going to be happy people. But managing these negative emotions reasonably well does not guarantee happiness; it only increases the probability of happiness.

No, happiness requires a bit more, something more proactive on our parts. In my counseling practice I noticed that most of my clients were not happy people. Happy people don't often seek counseling. When my clients and I examined their lives closely, I noticed that one factor stood out in their lives in almost every case: These unhappy people were not getting their *needs* met.

This book is not intended to be a psychology primer, but a little explanation of human needs, and how they relate to happiness, is in order.

The noted psychologist Abraham Maslow, Ph.D., explored this whole area and noted that humans have needs that have the following order of importance (9):

1) Physical: food, clothing, shelter, sex, etc.

2) Safety: feeling relatively free from harm

3) Love and belongingness: to be in intimate and close association with others

4) Self-esteem: feeling that we're important and okay

5) Self-actualization: that we're growing, exploring, and being all that we want to be

Some readers may not agree with Dr. Maslow, but his concepts have held up for many years and are followed by many professionals in their practices and teachings, and I have seen nothing in my many years of counseling that disproves them. In fact, I used to give my clients a *counseling guarantee* (something unheard of in the profession) that if they could get all these needs met in a reasonable fashion, they would then find themselves to be happy. Almost without exception, every client who used the counseling process to go forth in the world and get his or her needs met reported to me that he or she was happy. So let's assume that Dr. Maslow was on to something useful here and that his is a good general outline to follow. Any reader, who can embellish this as to his or her personal situation, should do so.

Thus, we can state affirmatively that *the pursuit of happiness is a process whereby people are working at and getting their needs met.* If they are not working at this process, or are failing at it, then they will report that they are not happy—perhaps depressed.

This means that you, the parents, must supply the needs of your children that are your responsibility and teach your children how to get those needs met that are their responsibility. If this all happens, you will then have happy children who will turn into happy adults. The critical point here is you must teach your children how to get their needs met for the rest of their lives.

The parents' most critical responsibility in their children's early developmental years is to provide proper food, clothing, and shelter; to keep them in a safe and secure environment; and to provide love and affection. Children need to be constantly told that they are "okay" as kids, both at home and in the community, by words and deeds. They need to be given the opportunity to grow and to prepare themselves to become responsible, useful adults. This process will produce happy children. And please remember, kids can't get too many hugs from parents and relatives or be told too often that they are loved!

This needs-gratification process is complicated and involved, and does contribute to happiness and emotional well-being, but we cannot go into all details of it in this chapter. Just remember that all aspects of the rest of this book address issues that contribute to your children's happiness.

CHAPTER 6

BEHAVIORAL AND SOCIAL SKILLS

In 1980, in a group discussion in my office, a social worker, my secretary, a recovering addicted physician, and I were discussing our low rate of success in our efforts to help addicted and mentally ill clients successfully complete our in-patient treatment program and assist them in transitioning successfully back to their communities. We were despondent because a recent follow-up survey showed that we weren't doing very well. Many of our patients/clients went back home and resumed their old self-defeating behaviors—that is, getting drunk, resuming drug use, and not working.

Of course, it wasn't us who were failing! After all, we were bright, educated people who were at the peak of the pyramid as far as knowledge and skills as to how to handle our clients' problems. We all did our jobs as well and thoroughly as possible. So why weren't we more successful?

After a while, my secretary pointed out that one problem she saw was that most of our clients weren't very attractive people. Many had poor hygiene, some of the women used bizarre patterns of makeup, and the men wore dirty, scruffy clothes. The conclusion was that most of them just didn't pass muster, as far as looks were concerned.

Another thing our group noticed was that many of the clients in the mental hospital lacked basic conversational skills. Many were silent and rarely spoke. Others were able to talk only about their physical ailments. Some could only complain about other people's shortcomings, while a few seemed to like the sound of their own voices, chattering on incessantly, never giving others a chance to voice their views. It became clear to us that old-fashioned conversational skills were in short supply, and we wondered if this defect had contributed to their current critical situations. In any event, we concluded that it would be helpful if they could learn to converse with others in a more appropriate fashion.

I had a very good colleague who was trained as a home economist, and she specialized in helping mental patients at our hospital learn conversational skills, personal hygiene, grooming, preparing and serving meals, and the other social graces. We began referring these patients to her as they progressed in their overall program and noticed that their mental health improved immensely. I became convinced that her services were more effective than the talk-therapy and medications. And wouldn't you know it, the ugly people got better looking by grooming themselves in a proper manner and becoming more sociable! The transformations were amazing (1)!

This line of thinking later got me to thinking about Otis, who had come to me one day in desperation, seeking advice on a very "personal" problem, as he put it, but which later proved to be the lack of a social skill.

"What's the problem?" I asked Otis as he settled into the chair beside my desk.

Otis had on a "new" Salvation Army-donated shirt and pants, about ten years out of fashion. He was about five foot eight and about forty pounds overweight. He had a friendly, cherubic-looking face and looked very much the part of the classic "good ole boy"—which he was! He was sixty-two years old.

"Well, Mr. Wilkins, as you know, I'm from the North Georgia mountains—born and raised there. And I'm in this here hospital for my drinking problem. First time I ever had to get treatment. Been here three weeks now, and my coordinator is Miss Smith. She's a real nice person, but I can't talk to her about this problem I got 'cause she's colored and a woman!"

"And you feel comfortable talking to me about it," I reflected.

"Well, I ain't comfortable talking to anybody 'bout it, but you're my best bet, I figger."

"Okay, tell me," I offered.

He lowered his head and turned as red as a man who'd just returned from a too-much-sun-and-beach vacation. Then he said, "As I said, I been here three weeks and I been given a week-end pass to go home and see my wife. We been married thirty-five years and got three growed children, and I really do want to see her."

"That's great, Otis, but what's the problem?"

He got redder and his lips thinner. Finally, he said, "Well...uh...My problem is I don't know how to do *it* sober!"

I was briefly confused. "Don't know how to do *what* sober?" I asked.

Now he was irritated. "You know," he shot back, "it!"

Then it dawned on me. "Oh...you mean sex!"

There was a large sigh from him now that I had mentioned the forbidden word. "Yeah, sex. I don't know how to do it sober. Never had sex with any woman lessen I was under the influence. And now I got to go back to my wife—horny as hell—and she's going to expect things out of me that I ain't never done sober!"

Now I was confused again. "Otis, you've been married thirty-five years and you're telling me that you and your wife have never had sex while you were sober?"

"That's right, Mr. Wilkins. But you and these other people here don't understand..." Then he jutted his face toward me and announced, "I ain't never done *nothing* sober!" Then he continued, "I had my first drink of liquor out of my daddy's moonshine still before I started school. I liked it so much I just kept on drinking it. I drank 'shine ever'day of my life, helping my daddy. When I went to school, I took a bottle with me. And when Daddy died and I took over the still, I kept on drinking, until I finally wound up in this place. Hell, I was drunk at my wedding, my mama's and daddy's funerals, and everything else in my life. And nobody knew I was drunk 'cause I could still do things pretty good. Besides, they'd never seen me any other way, so what'd they know?" Then he paused and looked at the ceiling. "Hell, I ain't never done nothing sober. I drank 'shine most ever'day of my life. And you ain't gonna believe this...My mama mixed 'shine with milk in my nipple bottle when I was a baby so I'd keep quiet and would sleep at night."

Well, I was flabbergasted with all this. I told Otis to go upstairs and get ready for his next group therapy session and I would work on his situation. I went to the nurses' station and reviewed his medical records, confirming all that he'd told me—except for the part about hardly ever having drawn a sober breath. But I knew he was telling the truth about that. And strangely enough, his wife was a devout Southern Baptist teetotaler!

Then I went to talk to his coordinator, Miss Smith, a social worker. We discussed his situation, and she agreed to call and talk to his wife. The call was made, and his wife confirmed all he'd told me, especially the part about him never having done anything sober as long as she had known him.

The social worker had explained to the wife that Otis would be coming home for the weekend to see her and reiterated what his concerns were about their impending sexual activities. To her surprise, the wife said that she understood and told her that she could handle the situation. Of course, we had our doubts, but we had no choice but to go along with the wife.

I then called Otis in and explained to him about the conversation between the social worker and his wife. He was enormously relieved. I then related to him some stories of other alcoholics who'd had similar problems in other areas of their lives, such as the salesman who'd never called on a prospect sober, but had to learn to do so after he got sober and how strange it felt at first, but it got easier the more he did it sober.

I concluded with this statement: "Otis, alcoholics who have done something for a long time while under the influence of alcohol always tell me that it feels different and scary when they quit drinking and now have to do those same things when they are stone-cold sober. It's as if I took you to a nudist camp and you had to walk around naked, because that's what they do there, but it was new to you—how do you think you'd feel?"

"Purty nervous 'cause I been wearing clothes all my life."

"Exactly, and that's what you've been doing with alcohol. It's been your 'social clothing' all your life, and for a while, you're going to feel naked without it. But if you stay sober, and work your AA program when you leave here, and keep doing what you have to, after a while you'll feel okay.

"Now, I'm giving you some homework when you go home this weekend. And your homework is to go home and have sex with your wife—stone-cold sober. Then you are to report back to me on Monday. Okay?"

He stood up then, puffed out his chest, and said, "I'll see you Monday, Mr. Wilkins," and then he turned and walked out.

When I walked into my office on Monday, there he was, smiling and still sober. I was relieved to see him sober, because I'd been fearful that he'd start drinking again. But he hadn't.

"Mr. Wilkins, you was right. Me and my wife got along real good," he said with a wide grin. "But, you know, it was real strange. It was like the first time I had sex—and it made me nervous. But we went on, and I don't think we're going to have any more problems."

After some further small talk, I wished him good luck. He subsequently completed our program at the hospital and returned home, stating that he was going to have to give up the moonshine business. I hope he did, because I never saw him again.

This story illustrates how a social skill (having sexual relations with one's spouse) can be totally different within one context as opposed to another. This is very common among people who abuse alcohol or drugs, but applies to other situations as well. For example, one may be well versed in confronting parents, but unable to do so with a boss. One may be quite comfortable in conversing with a stranger in a bar, a peer group, or relatives, but unable to talk in front of a group at work, ask a coach for more playing time, or ask a boss for a raise (2).

The point here is social skills are wide and varied, and just because your children are good in one area does not necessarily mean that they will be good in another. Many women are quite good at expressing themselves over a wide range of topics among like-minded women, but are helpless and inept emotionally at conversing with men about various subjects.

Young children need to learn how to talk and play with other boys and girls in a wide range of settings. And they especially need to do this while they're going through the difficult time of puberty. Many kids get into sex too early simply because they lack the social skills to handle the sexual tension that prevails among "hot-blooded" teens. The more socially adept teens, who have been properly trained by their parents, will handle this teenage sexual tension by emerging themselves in activities such as sports, hobbies, academics, and that old standby, masturbation. And whether they admit it or not, they need their parents' help in all this. (More about sex in Chapter 12.)

All this dictates that it is the parents' responsibility to teach and foster their childrens' learning as to proper grooming, hygiene, and conversational skills (including "small talk"), as well as learning how to behave around different races and ethnic groups, religions, and people in different economic and social strata. In the counseling business, we call this "the ability to communicate at all levels." Basically, you want your children to be able to get along with all the people they meet in their lives. This does not mean that they have to agree with or like them all, just get along in a socially approved manner.

Let's go into social behavior in more detail. These will be behaviors in which we engage with other people, more or less.

Most social behavior is what I call reflexive; that is, it arises out of our subjective thinking and past conditioning and is not necessarily well thought out at all. We just do it because that's the way we are. And as parents, we want to program this underlying genesis of day-to-day behavior in our children so that it habitually produces socially acceptable behaviors. We want to program our children with positive, constructive behaviors that they can rely on as adults, which will carry them through the good times and the bad—especially when their *thinking* and *feeling* systems are not functioning well.

Even so, we must realize that we all can behave in certain ways without any thought or feeling behind it. In the old Johnny Cash ballad, "Folsom Prison Blues," the subject in the song is lamenting his fate at being incarcerated in prison because he "...shot a man in Reno, just to watch him die..." illustrating the fact that people often act in negative ways *just to be doing it*, to see what it's like! All of us have committed bad deeds at times, just out of curiosity. This is one reason why we want to program those reflexive, socially good behaviors into our children to lessen the chance they will choose to experiment with more offensive, negative ones.

The following are social behaviors that your children will need to have in their repertoire, ones that can be relied upon day in and day out. This is not an exhaustive list, and you can subtract and add to it according to your own child-rearing philosophy. If your children can get to the age of eighteen or so with most of these skills, then they will be world-beaters, and the only thing left for you to do is to get out of their way!

Let's look at some common, important social behaviors:

SAYING NO: Many people cannot say no, even when they want to. Such folks tend to become doormats for other people, who soon detect this inability and abuse or overuse them. This deficiency is usually the result of over-conditioning by parents in an effort to raise "nice," complying children. The parents put so much social fear into their children that they are afraid to say no, because to do so usually leads to punishment or disapproval from the parents. The inability to say no when we need to is a big problem in our culture. It has been partially addressed by the teaching of *assertiveness*, but many students of this behavior have overdone it and learned to be *aggressive* rather than *assertive*, and aggressiveness usually gets one into trouble (3). (We will address this whole issue in Chapter 8, "Assertiveness Training.")

MANNERS: The use of good manners in all social situations cannot be overemphasized. I have never met anyone who got into trouble using good manners. Short of sending your little darlings to charm or finishing schools, like they did in the old days, parents are going to be the primary teachers here—as they will be in most of these social areas.

At an early age, you should teach your children to address their elders properly: Yes, ma'am; Yes, sir; Aunt Elsie; Granddaddy or Grandmamma; Mr. or Mrs.; and so on. If so instructed early on, it will become a part of their everyday behavior. It is my opinion, also, that children should not be encouraged to call their elders by their first names, as they do their playmates, because they might get the idea that they're more grown up than they are. Children are not the equals of adults.

And do teach your children good table manners: like chewing food with the mouth closed, how to converse at the dinner table, and how to speak in a conversational tone of voice. If, by chance, you do not know what good manners are (and I can't imagine any reader of this book being in ignorance here), then pick up a book on manners, or copy someone you know who has good manners. When your children display bad manners, explain the correct behavior to them and let them know what you expect of them. And above all, use good social behavior yourself so your children will have someone to copy. You are the most powerful teacher in this area.

You may think I am overemphasizing here, but let me relate a real-life situation. A client of mine once came to me complaining about being constantly passed over for promotions in his government job. He was a very bright, articulate, well-educated fellow, with a very agreeable, personal manner around people. It was hard to imagine why he was never seriously considered for promotions. One day after our counseling session, I invited him to lunch at our hospital cafeteria. We sat down to eat together, and what I observed shocked me!

He chewed his food with his mouth wide open and talked at the same time—spewing particles of food all over the table. At our next counseling session, I confronted him on this behavior and asked him if maybe this didn't have something to do with him being passed over for promotions, especially since he often went to lunch with colleagues and bosses. As you might guess, he was unaware of this behavior, saying he'd always eaten that way, but no one had ever said anything about it except for his ex-wife, and he'd figured she was just venting her anger toward him! After further discussion, we concluded he should change this behavior immediately—which he did—and a year later he was promoted to section chief at his job! Let's hear one for good table manners!

A big part of manners in general is children have to learn that mannerly behavior arises out of respect for other people. If your children see you treating others respectfully, they will likewise. And when they have problems with their playmates, do not assume that your little precious ones are the victims; many times it will be them who are the predators. But they will learn a lot if you intervene on these occasions to get at the source of the problem and resolve it in a fair manner. And if your children are at fault, some sort of discipline will likely be in order. This will predispose your children to begin to think of others as being just as important in the large scheme of things as they are—and good manners will follow.

Other members of your family and circle of friends will be involved in manners training as well. When I was about ten years old and beginning to feel more "grown up," my family was visiting my father's sister, Kema, and her husband, Kell, and I proceeded to address them by their first names only, dropping the "Aunt" and "Uncle." Well, my Uncle Kell picked up on that immediately and took me aside and said, "Look, Joey, that lady in the kitchen is not 'Kema' to you. I call her Kema, your daddy calls her 'Kema,' your mama calls her 'Kema,' but you are going to call her '*Aunt* Kema.' And you call me '*Uncle* Kell.' Understand?"

Well, of course I understood. I had meant no harm, but by the determined look in Uncle Kell's eyes, I knew I'd better do as he said if I wanted to stay in his good graces, which I wanted to do, because he was always doing good things for me. And I didn't want to mess that up. So from then on, it was "Aunt" and "Uncle" with them and all my other aunts and uncles as well.

GETTING ALONG WITH OTHERS: This is a critical skill for your children to have, with family members, coworkers, neighbors, and even strangers. And getting along with others is more of an attitude than anything else. So your task as parents is to inculcate a positive attitude toward others in your children.

A good place to start is to teach them the Golden Rule: *Do unto others as you would have them do unto you.* The Golden Rule is universal; it is promoted by all the major religions in one form or another. It is also the basis for most secular, humanistic behavior, whether it is conserving energy, saving the environment, or Kumbayah get-togethers. If you accept the premise that all human beings deserve a fair shake in life, as espoused in the Declaration of Independence, the Constitution, and the U.N. Universal Declaration of Human Rights, then why wouldn't you want to treat others as you would like to be treated? The only exception to this would be those who don't follow the Golden Rule, break the law, or commit gross social misdeeds. But we have police, judges, and prison systems to take care of these offenders. The rest are best handled with assertive behavior (as outlined in Chapter 8).

Once you have taught your children the Golden Rule by *your* words and deeds, many of their other behavioral and social skills will be taught by their church, school, and other positive, social activities. They'll learn many lessons by participating in group activities in which they have an interest. School bands and orchestras are great for this. Participating in Girl or Boy Scouts, 4-H, and similar activities can't be beaten. Children with a flair for the dramatic can engage in school plays, where all have an interdependent role.

I am a great believer that most children should participate in team sports, from Little League on up, commensurate with their interests and abilities. I think it's no coincidence that women in our society have become more assertive and outspoken in the last few decades as opportunities have opened up for them to participate in more types of sports during their developmental years. There's a world of difference between the modern woman and those a few generations back, who had very few sports in which to participate.

In addition to learning to get along with and appreciating others on the athletic field, sports introduce to children the payoff that comes from physical activity, which can establish good long-term habits. People who get plenty of physical activity are generally healthier and happier. However, children need to be reminded that they are participating in sports not just to win, but to learn all the benefits that come from these activities. And it will be your responsibility to ensure that your children do get to participate, and not become chronic "bench warmers." If your children can't do well in one activity, take them out and get them into one in which they can do well. And watch out for overzealous coaches who think they're managing the Atlanta Braves and that your child is the next Babe Ruth or, conversely, the worst substitute that nobody ever heard of. Again, your assertive skills will come in handy here.

Both of my children were required to participate in group activities all through school. And they had to play at least one team sport. They were allowed to pick the activities and sports, and flip-flopped around a bit, but they enjoyed these activities and learned many social skills that hold them in good stead to this day. Their mother and I backed them all the way. You should do no less.

RELATIONSHIPS WITH AUTHORITIES: How many people do you know who have problems getting along with authority figures? It seems to be a universal problem that many people just don't like to have a boss over them. This usually arises from bad parenting during the children's formative years, though some personalities seem naturally inclined this way. If children have bad feelings about their parents, then why would they view other authority figures any differently? But the reality is everyone has a "boss," telling them what to do, what rules they must follow, regulating them, having superior knowledge, etc. So it's critical that you teach your children how to fit themselves into a world where, when they look up, there's always someone "over" them. In my work with chronic homeless people over the years, I have observed that one trait many of them have is an inability to get along with authority figures. Lack of this social skill dooms many of them to a life of despair and isolation and an inability to work. (4). And you've doubtless heard the old saying, "There are too many chiefs and not enough Indians!" Well, it's my contention that many want to be chiefs, because they haven't learned how to be properly submissive to authority when the need arises.

The best and most important place to start is with you. First, you are already the most important authority figures in your children's lives. And how you handle your authority situations will set a lifetime pattern in your children. As the "boss" of your child, it is important that you convey in a firm, but caring way that you are the authority. Your control is absolute. You set the rules in the house, with the children following them as you require. This will protect your children and get good behavior started. Later, as the children mature, you can negotiate some of the rules when they are able to rationally present their case as to why those rules may need modification. Try not to become overly rigid with your children. If you become a non-negotiable person with them, they are probably going to tune you out in all areas.

If you have done a good job with your children before puberty, you will then be better prepared to assert your authority during the turbulent teenage years. And I might add that some children become very difficult to manage as teenagers. Often, bad peer influences, combined with certain personality traits of the children, contribute to difficult-to-manage teens.

So you may ask, "I've done all those things you've mentioned, but my kid's now fourteen years old and won't do a thing I ask her to. She's acting very irresponsibly, giving only minimal effort in her schoolwork and doing the opposite of what I want her to. What can I do?"

The first thing you can do is to stay as calm and rational as possible. You and your spouse should discuss it and then discuss it with your children. Point out the bad behavior and the trouble it's causing. Let your children know how it makes you feel: mad, sad, or afraid. Be honest here. Show some empathy by illustrating how you may have had similar problems with your parents, and the ill will and problems that arose because of it. Evaluate whether your children have gotten into alcohol or drugs. If so, seek professional help. However, please remember that if your children are using alcohol or drugs, and you ask them about it, they're most likely going to lie to you about it;

it goes with the territory. So you'll have to look for hard evidence here, confront them, and refer them for treatment.

A lot of your children's attitudes toward authority figures will come from their experiences with teachers; after all, they're with teachers six or so hours a day—maybe more than with you. So it's important that they learn how to relate to these teachers.

As you already know, the school system in America is one of our most organized institutions, and the role of administrators, teachers, and pupils is pretty much known to all. The trick is for you not to make it look bad in your children's eyes. How do you do this? By joining the PTA and becoming an active participant. Also, consult with your children's teachers when needed and let them know that you support their work with your children. Ask what you can do at home to reinforce their work. Go to the functions put on by the school at the beginning of each year, designed to acclimate parents and pupils to the school and its personnel. Let your children see you doing this. And never berate teachers or the school in front of your children. If you have a serious concern, schedule a special conference with the appropriate school personnel to work things out. The bottom line is you must instill in your children, by your words and deeds, that you, the children, and the school system are a team and that you expect your children to be good team players. The children should feel that if they are not good school team players, there will be serious consequences from you. If you can get this idea in your children's minds, you are likely to have very few problems in this regard, and your children will do a better job of learning what the school has to offer.

PEER RELATIONSHIPS: Closely watch your children's associations with peers. Listen to what these peers have to say about the teachers and the school system in general. If your children begin to be overly influenced by their peers in a negative manner, you will probably need to remove them from such influences. This is probably one of the most pervasive problems regarding hostile or indifferent attitudes facing American school systems today, especially during students' teen years. All schools have a core of disgruntled, hostile students, who try to promote the idea that the learning process in school is not "cool," and they try to recruit as many to their point of view as they can. Make sure that your children are not part of their recruits. Encourage your children to associate with those peers who value school and the learning process.

When my son was in second grade, he was assigned to some special remedial classes to improve his diction. Testing had shown that he had a slight lisp, and his teachers felt he needed to overcome this. His mother and I agreed, so he was assigned to these classes. However, this took him out of some regular classes, and one boy in his homeroom class, feeling a need to belittle him about this, began to "pick on him," hitting him when the teachers weren't around. It was the classic case of the school bully, not submissive to the school system, trying to exert his anger, for whatever reason, on those he perceived to be weaker. I did not want my son to be intimidated by this boy nor to feel inferior for going to his special classes where he was learning a better way to speak.

As the first course of action, I told him to be assertive and have a serious talk with this bully and tell him to stop, or he'd be reported to the teacher. This didn't work, so my son went to the teacher. However, she was unable to fully control the bully, because he began hitting my son in the boys' bathroom, where there were no teachers to observe. At this point, I knew from my own experience that there are times when one simply must deal with a bully on his or her own. But my son had been taught that it was wrong to go around hitting people, and since he was a compliant child,

I knew I was going to have to give him permission to go to the next step.

"Son, you're dealing with a bully here," I began. "I don't know why this kid's hitting you. He's probably insecure, got problems at home—whatever. But it's got to stop. Do you agree?"

He nodded yes.

"Well, you've asked him to stop and he won't. You've gone to the teacher and she hasn't been able to make him stop. So you're going to have to make him stop. The next time he hits you, I want you to hit him back. Can you do that?"

He said he could, and I continued, "I always want you to be assertive first when someone is trying to hurt you, by asking them to stop whatever they're doing, but if they don't stop, then you've got to get aggressive and use force. And if you get into any trouble because of this, I'll be down at your school taking care of the situation."

A few days later, my son come to me and reported, "I took care of that bully, Dad. He won't hit me anymore."

"What happened?" I asked.

"Well, we were in the boy's bathroom, and he starting saying nasty things and hitting on me. And I told him if he didn't stop I was going to hit him back. But he didn't stop, so I hit him in the stomach *seven* times, and he fell down on the floor. Then I left him there."

Needless to say, my son had no more trouble with that bully. And there must have been other boys in the bathroom observing all this, because my son developed the reputation around the school as someone not to meddle with. And he never had any more such problems all through his school years.

I can hear it now. Some of you parents will be appalled by my advice to my son. You probably think I should have taken further steps with the school administration. But life is short, and even the best schools sometimes can't handle those situations that ultimately have to be dealt with by the students themselves. And if I'd stepped in further, my son would have gotten a reputation that he was a special kid that had to be rescued by his dad and the teachers and couldn't take care of himself. What a wimp! There are no wimps in this family—and you don't want them in yours.

ATTITUDES TOWARD SCHOOL: Despite all the rhetoric about America's poor public schools, low SATs, disinterested teachers, and the like, the fact is most people are teaching because they want to teach. Strange as it may seem to the rest of us, most teachers like their jobs! And they enjoy students who want to learn. When teachers get students who are doing their assignments and working hard at their studies, then you'll have students and teachers who will work well together.

Basically, your task is to teach your children to have a positive attitude about learning in general, teaching them that, no matter who the teacher is, they can learn something from even a bad teacher if they just stick to their goals, work hard, and make the effort that is required. Children have to feel that *the worse their learning situation is the more determined they have to become.* Nobody's going to stop them from learning just because they got a clunker of a teacher this year. Of course, if the situation gets too bad, you should intervene with the teacher or the principal.

When my daughter was in third grade, she began to have problems with one of her teachers. Things were not going well, she reported, but I wasn't clear as to the specifics. I had met her teacher at the beginning of the year and wasn't too impressed, because the woman seemed nervous talking to my wife and me, and appeared somewhat disoriented, or scatterbrained, if you will. But we figured she was new on the job and would calm down and do an acceptable job. But, apparently, that was not happening.

So we sat my daughter down and, using supportive-type questioning, began to get a hint as to what the problem was. My daughter wasn't getting enough individual attention from the teacher when she needed it in some difficult areas involving math. My daughter also began to sense that she was being neglected because she was white (the teacher was a female African American). When I asked her how she got that impression, she stated that she spent all her time with the black kids and let the white ones struggle in silence on their own.

Well, you can imagine our consternation. Were we going to have a racial incident here—start up a white civil rights movement? After I cooled down, I saw that we needed to tread lightly, lest we hurt our daughter more. So I wrote a brief note to the teacher requesting a meeting, saying that my daughter and I would be discussing the problem with her, but that I expected the *two of them* to work things out, and I would remain in the background, observing.

Then my daughter and I wrote out a little speech to make to the teacher, stating the problem and the help she needed. My daughter rehearsed and memorized the speech, then took the note to the teacher. I immediately followed this up with a phone message to the teacher to set a time for our appointment, again emphasizing that my daughter would be doing most of the talking and that I was having her do this in order for her to develop her assertiveness skills. When we met with the teacher, my daughter assertively stated her problem with learning the math and that she needed some additional help. Well, the teacher was very embarrassed and apologetic—and most eager to help, which she later did. There were no more problems between my daughter and this teacher.

However, had I not intervened, my eight-year-old daughter would have passively done nothing, her learning needs would have gone unmet, and the whole third grade experience would have likely programmed her into negative attitudes about the entire learning experience in general, and mathematics specifically. As an aside, she went on to become very proficient in math and got a BS degree in applied mathematics in college.

So please take note: Your children need you to be involved in their education—and so does the school system!

TIMELINESS: Teach your children to always be on time! Nothing is more aggravating than waiting for tardy people.

I once attended a conference on racial issues with which counselors needed to be aware. The presenter was an African American man who stated that white counselors needed to be aware of CPT: "colored people time." CPT, as he explained it, was different than the time-schedules that most educated white folks followed, and if we didn't understand it and make the necessary adjustments, we would be in for a lot of frustration in dealing with our African American clients. As he explained it, the main issue with CPT that we counselors needed to understand was that when we scheduled these clients for a 2:00 p.m. appointment, say, we couldn't necessarily expect him or her to be there at that time. Rather, the clients were most likely to be there "around 2:00 p.m.," which, in their frame of reference, could mean any time between lunch and supper!

Well, I was somewhat skeptical, but in the ensuing months, my African American clients proved him to be right, more or less. Many of these clients would arrive long before or after—usually after—their appointment times, with explanations that seldom made sense. I soon realized I was dealing with some sort of sociological phenomenon within the African American community, over which I had limited power to change. I tried several things with scheduling systems, but they didn't work. After much struggle—because I had a lot of clients who were unable to be at my office at their designated times—I evolved a solution.

When clients came early, I made them wait until the appointment time, even though I may have been able to see them earlier. Sometimes they would wait, and sometimes they would leave. But the next time they were always punctual. For those who were late, I wouldn't see them on that day, offering to reschedule them another day. For those who rescheduled, they were always prompt the next time.

This technique worked nearly 100 percent of the time, and it will work with your children, too.

When our son was just starting first grade, my wife was having trouble getting him out to wait for the school bus on time. She always had to push and cajole him to get moving so he wouldn't miss the bus. Well, this morning ritual was getting tiresome fast. No matter what she did, he couldn't be speeded up; threats of punishment and taking away privileges were tried, but nothing worked.

Then, one morning, she decided to try something new: She was going to let him be late for the bus, get left behind, and see what happened! Sure enough, the next day, he was dawdling again as usual. But my wife said nothing, and as expected, he didn't get to the bus stop in time, and the bus left just as he was strolling out the front door. He immediately ran back into the house in a panic, but my wife stayed calm and let him stew for a while. She wanted him to get the full emotional impact of what it felt like to be late. After a few hours of him being in a very nervous state, she finally put him in the car and took him to school, where he had to suffer the embarrassment of being late with his schoolmates—and having to be brought to school by his mother! Not too good for a macho first grader!

From that date forward, our son was never again late. He immediately began getting out to the bus stop early, with no prompting from his mother. And to this day, he is always on time for his appointments with customers, family, and friends. That one incident was all it took to change that evolving always-late behavior.

Being on time is important. It shows discipline on your children's part and respect for others, both very good qualities for all children to have. Again, modeling on your part is important. If your children are late, then let natural consequences take effect. If you tell your children you'll take them to a movie at 4:00 and they're not ready, leave without them. I guarantee they'll be ready the next time. And the younger you do this with your children, the less likely you'll have to repeat it, as you might with a teenager, simply because young children will not have yet developed the convoluted reasoning and blaming-others behavior at which older children can become quite skilled. However, this technique will also work with most adults, to the extent that their relationship with you is important.

COURTESY ON THE ROAD: Being a good driver is a matter of driver education and individual temperament on the road. Teach your children these things by letting them see you behaving as a good driver, obeying the laws, holding your speed down, and being courteous to other drivers. When you see other drivers breaking the rules of the road, point it out to your children and instruct them as to the right way. With fourteen years or so watching Mom and Dad being good drivers, they'll at least have a foundation on which to base their instruction when they begin their driver's education, whether it's from you, school, or private instruction.

The most critical thing that besets young drivers, which costs too many of them their lives, is ignorance of the laws of motion of heavy moving vehicles. Young people just do not know how quickly they can get in trouble at high speeds. In a flash, someone can cut in front of them, or the tires slip on a wet road, and the next thing you know they're dead. A good trick that I've observed is to take your children to a deserted area of a large parking lot when it has ice on it (if you live up North). Drive at a slow speed—and then slam on the breaks. The car will slide and spin, and your children will either be scared or think it's a lot of fun. In any event, you can point out how this can happen on ice, on wet pavement, or hot asphalt with just a little bit of moisture on it. And while it may be gory and brutal, observing bad wrecks has an impact on children. And do teach your children not to follow too closely, that the expressways are not the Daytona 500! I can't tell you how many teen-aged children of my friends and clients have been killed in automobile accidents, primarily because they were unaware how quickly disaster can occur at high speeds for given conditions.

OVER-EMPOWERMENT OF CHILDREN: This is going to be a touchy subject with some parents. The tendency in our society since World War II by enlightened, conscientious parents has been to elevate children's self-esteem to levels unheard of in previous generations. It has resulted in adults who think of themselves first and foremost. They behave as if all of society should meet their every wants and desires. They believe they should have the perfect home, spouse, job, salary, medical care, retirement benefits, etc. Their children must get into a prestigious private high school and col-lege.

Children raised with this orientation tend to expect the best for themselves and are often in despair or depressed when things don't work out as they would like. They have trouble handling personal suffering, because their parents protected them from it as much as possible. Basically, these children are overprotected and catered to, and have not struggled with life problems to the extent that they could have learned some things in those struggles.

The question then remains as to what causes this orientation.

Recently, while meditating and praying in church, a young child's crying and wailing interrupted my congregation. Do you think the parents removed the child? They did not, choosing to futilely try to hush the child—succeeding only after several minutes and destroying the mood of the entire service. Why these parents would take an infant into the main service when we have an excellent nursery to care for such children, allowing the parents to better get their spiritual needs met instead of being preoccupied with a crying baby, is sad, indeed. Obviously, they were neglecting their needs to fulfill some imagined duty to make sure their child was getting something the nursery couldn't provide. Or something like that.

On another occasion in a church I was visiting, two young girls about six years of age got up in front of the congregation and began prancing back and forth, just below the pulpit, while the pastor was delivering his sermon. And the parents did nothing except watch in amusement at their precocious children! Of course, the congregation couldn't remember a word the preacher said!

Afterward, when my wife asked the pastor why he didn't do something, he replied they didn't bother him, so he continued his sermon! Unbelievable!

It's abundantly clear that recent generations of parents have abandoned that old bromide that children should be seen and not heard. Probably the strongest evidence of this is in many of our professional athletes when they celebrate ostentatiously after scoring or doing something magnificent on the field of play. There is very little modesty and a lot of "trash talk."

When children get too much of a good thing during their formative years, such as freedom to feel equal to adults in thought, word, and deed, and are enthusiastically rewarded for it, what can we expect when they grow up? My thesis is children should have good self-esteem, but not at the expense of deference and respect to their parents, teachers, and the society at large. So don't overdo the self-esteem thing!

CHAPTER 7

TOUGH LOVE

Tough love, as used here, is presented as the ability to sympathize *and* empathize with other people's problems, while at the same time being able to detach yourself enough so that you will be able to rationally and objectively act in ways that the situation demands. To put it another way, it's the ability to remain cool and calm in a crisis so that you can do what you have to do.

Some examples are as follows:

1) When your children have severe injuries, you are able to stay calm, sooth their hysteria, and get them to proper medical attention.

2) When your children have to be disciplined for a misdeed, you are able to stay calm

and detached, administer the discipline, and control your own anger.

3) When your children come to you at age twelve saying they are going out on a date—but you know they're not ready for such an experience—you remind them of the family rule (which has been previously discussed with them) that there will be no dating until age sixteen (or whatever age you think appropriate).

4) When your children want to spend their money on a video game that you consider too violent, you refuse their desires.

5) When your children want to go swimming with their buddies in an area that you know is dangerous—with no lifeguards—you refuse.

You will note that some of the aspects of tough love behavior will, of necessity, make your children go through some anger and frustration when they don't get their way, coupled with all the fall-out that you are sure to get whenever you refuse their wishes. But as the old-timers used to say, "It's for your own good!" And it usually is.

The first places I heard of tough love were at Alcoholic Anonymous meetings and with other mental health staff in the treatment of addicts and mental patients. No doubt the phrase was coined years ago by some recovering alcoholic who was perhaps sponsoring a manipulative client who may have wanted to get sober, but insisted on doing it "his way," as opposed to following the rigorous AA twelve-step recovery process. And people who are trying to help addicts get clean and sober have learned over the years that there is no shortcut, or "free lunch," as they often call it. So they insist that their clients do it the way that has been proven beneficial over the years with millions of addicted people. This is tough love (1).

In child rearing, most parents intuitively know what their children *should* do, but often, these parents are led astray by changing social customs, permissive media, and loosening moral standards. Also, many exasperated teachers have given up and no longer demand excellence of their pupils, using all kinds of rationales to justify easy A's and social promotions, with the students and some parents believing that's the way things ought to be.

Tough love makes demands on parents that usually compromises their time and energy. Tough love is not easy to do. It requires emotional stamina and extra time from the parents. It's especially easier for parents to give in to children if those parents have to work outside the home or are single parents. Administering tough love can make parents seem like mean, non-caring people sometimes, especially to those other parents and child rearers who don't practice it.

Tough love is for loving, dedicated, caring, disciplined parents who know what they are doing. If you are faint of heart and are not able to administer it, then your children will suffer later.

Let me give you a very dramatic example of tough love, as administered in the U.S. Marine Corps, an organization in which one would not expect to find it. This is a true story, experienced by one of my friends, and it illustrates special circumstances where the Marines had to finish the job that a young Marine recruit's parents didn't (2).

The Marine Corps sends all new recruits to Parris Island, South Carolina, for their basic training—or for physical and "attitude adjustment" services, as my friend calls it. And these recruits come from all over the country, from all walks of life: different races, educational backgrounds, and socioeconomic situations. They're about as diverse a group as you could find. And these men and women present a special problem to the Marine Corps: In just twelve weeks, the Corps has to get all these different personalities working cohesively together, there being little room for individualism in their groups. The realities they will face in future combat situations dictate they leave their personal idiosyncrasies behind and work together in disciplined units to engage the enemy and defend each other.

Seems like an impossible task, doesn't it? Especially in view of the fact that many of our well-established organizations, which have the need to get people to behave in certain ways in which they resist, are unable to do so—like families that can't get children to behave, parole boards that can't get newly released prisoners to obey the law, welfare agencies that can't get people to quit having babies they can't take care of, treatment facilities that can't get addicts to stay clean and sober, and abused women who can't get their wretched husbands to stop beating them. Believe me, the Marine Corps knows how to shape a varied group of men and women into cohesive action quickly. And they do it by using tough love!

So the tough love model shows that there is a way to control such resistant behaviors if we will only muster up the gumption to administer it. While you and I have little control over the larger society's will in this area, you parents have all the power you need in regard to your own children. However, please understand that I am not advocating abuse of your children; just setting the limits and letting reasonable consequences follow misbehavior.

The year was 1967 and the war in Vietnam was "cooking." The Marines needed new men in large numbers—fast—to go fight in an unpopular war, which most of the recruits wished they could avoid. For one particular platoon, it was the tenth week of their basic training, with only two weeks to go. Most of the men seemed to be doing well and were looking forward to graduation and becoming full-fledged Marines.

"Everyone fall out tomorrow for a twenty-mile, forced march," announced their drill instructor. "I want full field packs—with helmets, *extra boots*, double ammo, and full canteens. Don't leave anything behind, because you're going to need all your gear. I want you fully outfitted and prepared for anything that might come up. Are there any questions?" There were none. Everyone knew what they had to do.

The next morning, off they marched, each man loaded down with over fifty pounds of gear, headed for a beach, several miles away. It was very hot and humid. After an exhausting march, they arrived at the beach, feet hurting, with their packs seeming to weigh hundreds of pounds. The men had been resting for a few moments when a truck rumbled up alongside the platoon and stopped.

"Okay," the drill instructor barked out, "rest a minute and drink lots of water. Then take off your boots and tie them together with these tags I'm handing out. Put your last name and serial number on the tags and throw the boots on that truck. Then get out your spare boots and put 'em on. We'll be marching back in five minutes."

Immediately, the men hustled to comply with his command—except for one man. This lone recruit just stood there, looking hopeless and lost. The drill instructor noticed him immediately and yelled in his face, "What's wrong, Marine? Didn't you hear me? Tag those boots!"

"But, sir, I can't," he blurted out in desperation.

"And why not?" bellowed the drill instructor.

"Because I didn't bring my extra boots," he answered sheepishly.

The drill instructor had seen this behavior before, whereby recruits would leave out some equipment from their packs in order to make them lighter and make their hike easier. He put his arms on his hips and jutted his face inches from the recruit's, as if getting ready for combat.

"Well, that's just too bad, Marine. You should have brought those extra boots like you were instructed, because you're going to need them. Off with those boots—now!"

The recruit was really desperate now. "But, sir," he implored, "I'll have to march back barefooted."

The drill instructor was unimpressed with his pleading, and replied, "Well, that's just too bad. You should have done as you were ordered. Now, tag those boots!" he screamed.

The recruit immediately sat down and hurriedly removed his boots. He looked around at the others, but could see he was getting no sympathy from them.

Then the platoon began the long march back. They hiked through scrubs and briars, palmettos and sandburs, and on hot asphalt and concrete. The drill instructor intentionally made the trip back much more difficult, causing our barefooted recruit all the pain you might imagine.

After a few torturous miles, the recruit could take no more and he dropped out of formation on the side of the road, while the others marched on. He was then ordered into the truck and taken straight to the brig, where he was locked up for several days, wondering nervously what was going to happen to him. However, after the drill instructor thought the recruit had learned his lesson, he was allowed to rejoin his platoon. He was a model recruit after that experience.

As you can see, the young recruit learned his lesson well—and fast! Very few words were exchanged. No attempts were made to find out why he had left his boots behind. He was not referred to a counselor to determine the reasons for his rebellion and passive-aggressive behavior. No attempt was made to reason with him, as most of us would be prone to do. There was no getting the other men involved, other than they only observed his dilemma and how it was dealt with. This was a simple case of "If you don't do what I tell you to, then certain consequences will follow." Tag your boots!

I know, some of you readers are thinking that the drill instructor was too harsh, that the punishment was cruel and oppressive, and that this is not an example of tough love. It may be tough, but where's the love?

Well, from the drill instructor's (or a parent's) perspective, he knew these men were likely going to be called into combat in the jungles of Vietnam, and if they were going to survive that ordeal, they would need rigorous discipline, precise combat skills, and the ability to work together as a unit. If any Marine decided he was going to do it *his* way, he would be jeopardizing his and his comrades' lives. And there was only a brief amount of time to prepare these men for this upcoming ordeal. So how more loving can you be than to give to others what you know they'll need in the way of training, in hopes of them doing their jobs well and coming out alive? Don't you think that's what your children are going to need as they face the trials and tribulations of life? And that's tough love.

I'm not saying that you have to be drill instructors to administer tough love to your children, but a milder version of the process will be good for them and will prepare them for some of the hard knocks they will run into later in life. And if you raise them with both soft love and tough love, when they leave the nest these behaviors will be a part of their personalities and they'll be able to administer and receive both types of love.

Some parents of my acquaintance had a twelve-year-old boy who had received $50 for a Christmas gift from his grandparents. He was anxious to spend the money on a present, so his father took him to a shopping mall where they went into an electronics store. The boy picked out an electronic game that the father quickly saw was too complex for the boy, but the father was unable to dissuade the boy from purchasing it. The father said that he was torn between letting the boy spend the money as he wished or refusing him, knowing that he would not be able to use the game properly. Finally, the father said his son could buy it, but he would have to keep it—he could not return it if he didn't like it. The son agreed.

When they returned home with the game, the boy took the game to his room and proceeded to try to play it. But Dad had been right; it was too complicated for him, so the son bounded downstairs and insisted they return it so he could get his money back. Dad swallowed hard and said no, reminding the son of their agreement.

With this, the son went into a rage, ran back upstairs and destroyed the game, wasting the whole $50 purchase.

Immediately, Dad and Mom went into conference, and they decided to exercise some tough love. They devised a written behavioral contract, outlining his inappropriate behavior, setting his punishment, and explaining why he was being punished. The son was told he had to agree to the contract, sign it, and follow the contract requirements, which promoted corrective behavior. The son saw that his parents were in total agreement on this and there was no way that he could "wiggle" out. So, after a short period of contemplation and struggling with his emotions, the son reluctantly complied and signed, eventually fulfilling the contract.

The boy learned his lesson the hard way and the parents had no further such problems with their son. Tag your boots!

CHAPTER 8

ASSERTIVENESS TRAINING

The most important interpersonal skill that you can teach your children is for them to be able to act assertively when the need arises. Assertive people are able to stand up for themselves by speaking out and acting in a socially approved manner in order to get their needs met. And, as we have previously noted, people who are getting their needs met are happy people (1).

I was introduced to assertiveness training in 1973, in a special post-master's counseling course of study at the Georgia Mental Health Institute, by my major professor, Stan Smits, Ph.D., and by Harold Haddle, Ph.D., the main presenter. He was presenting this course to a selected group of vocational rehabilitation counselors as a new way to develop positive behavioral skills in our clients, enabling them to better function in their everyday lives. At that time, I had a caseload of about 150 clients, all of whom had been hospitalized at this institute for either mental illness or alcohol and/or drug addiction. And, sad to say, I was not making much progress with these folks as far as getting them back to their communities to resume normal, productive living.

This assertiveness training looked promising to me, so I thought I'd give it a try. Certainly, the traditional psychiatric and counseling treatment was not doing enough, so I went to my unit chief and got her permission to start a new type of counseling group, in hopes of leading people out of their despair, to return to their homes and work. She was somewhat doubtful about my ability to do this with such a new type of therapy, but she was as anguished as I was over our low rate of success, so, with her permission, I formed a counseling group of twelve patients, and we started meeting twice weekly.

And the results were amazing. Of those patients who learned these new assertive behavioral principles and began to act assertively on their own behalf (all but three), there followed a great deal of improvement as to their general moods, with much less depression and negative thinking. Some even became optimistic and cheerful (2)!

Why did this technique work when others had failed? With assertiveness training, they could recognize and identify with a style of behavior that was simple, readily understandable, easy to do, and got immediate results. Almost without exception, these patients were people who had been taught to "stuff" their feelings of anger, to keep quiet and endure whatever misfortune life threw at them, and after all that, when they became volcanoes of anger, ready to explode, they would erupt with a flow of negative emotions and behavior that would get them into trouble with their family and friends, and occasionally, the law. Many had also tried to anesthetize themselves with alcohol and drugs over the years, in a futile attempt to put out the volcanic fires within. But all that did was make it easier to explode when they were under the influence of alcohol or their drug of choice. We have all experienced the poor quiet soul who never says a cross word to anyone while clean and sober, but who becomes a torrent of rage when drunk. People of this type are trapped by their own anger and don't know what to do about it. You can imagine the joy my clients felt when someone came along who offered some hope of getting out of this psychological dilemma.

Based on this beginning success, I incorporated assertiveness training into my traditional counseling program with all my clients who needed it. Over a counseling career spanning thirty years, I have taught several thousand individual clients, and even more mental health and other professional staff, on how to use this technique. So successful was this that I began to give my clients a guarantee of success, something unheard of in counseling circles. I said to all, "If you will learn and apply these principles in your daily life, I guarantee you things will get better. If you try them and things don't get better, I want you to come back and tell me." No one ever came back!

Of course, I realize that some tried these principles and may have failed, and were probably too shy or insecure about reporting their failures to me, but in those instances where I followed up, all clients reported that things had gotten better—not perfect, but better. And all professional staff who I trained reported that the clients they in turn trained, did better as well.

All you readers have probably heard of assertiveness training, but you are likely a little fuzzy on the details. And some of you may have assertive behavior confused with aggressive behavior. There's a big difference.

So let's get down to the basics. The assertiveness model says that there are three styles of behavior: *nonassertive*, *aggressive*, and *assertive* (3).

Nonassertive people basically don't take care of themselves; they don't secure their own basic rights and needs. They tend to be inhibited, feel hurt, and are anxious most of the time. They don't choose options for themselves, allowing others to choose for them, be it parents, teachers, bosses, friends, etc. They may have goals they'd like to achieve, but usually don't, falling short for a variety of convenient excuses and feeling worse about themselves every day. Underlying all this *nonassertive* behavior is a sense of unworthiness and low self-esteem. They are the wallflowers of our society. They are much more prone to becoming depressed and mentally ill than others (4).

Aggressive people are at the other extreme. They tend to think the world revolves around them. They like to be the center of attention. They don't care much for other people's feelings. They are usually very expressive and outspoken. They choose *for* other people and usually *do* achieve their goals—but hurt others in the process. They depreciate others and tend to put the other person down. Carried to the extreme, these people often get in trouble with the law. They have few close friends (5).

Assertive people are the best at taking care of themselves and achieving their goals, and their goals are usually more socially acceptable. They know what their rights are and how to keep others from trampling on those rights. They are good at announcing who they are and what they want, yet they do it in a way that is not overbearing or offensive. They are sensitive to other people's feelings and know how to get their needs met in a socially approved manner—even on those occasions when others might not like it. And because they are skilled at all this, they usually feel good about themselves (6).

So, after looking at these three styles of behavior, which do you want for your children? It's really a no-brainer, isn't it? What parents wouldn't want their children to be primarily assertive people? Assertive behavior is based upon the premise that all human beings have certain inalienable rights, and three of the most important ones are as follows:

The right to make a reasonable request of someone else

The right to refuse an unreasonable request of someone else that does not meet your desires or needs

The right to correct a wrong done to you by others

In order for one to accomplish these rights, it has been found by psychologists and other researchers of human behavior that these rights can best be achieved by responding to other people in an appropriate, assertive manner. To do this, your children will need to learn to make assertive responses to others when the need arises (7).

Assertive statements have three components to them: *empathy*, *content*, and *action* (8). But before we go further, we need to understand clearly just what empathy is.

Empathy is *not* sympathy. Empathy is the ability to put oneself in other people's shoes and to make a reasonable guess as to what they are *thinking* and *feeling*. This means you have to learn to stop and think about other people's behavior and not over-react aggressively when they do something you don't like. You may have to suspend many of your own feelings and thoughts for a while, until you figure out what's going on with that other person. For example, suppose you come home to your wife, and for no reason that you can readily detect, she starts criticizing your neighbor, whom you really like, and this makes you angry. Rather than lashing back at her and pointing out the flaws of all her girlfriends—being the astute, knowledgeable, assertive person that you are—you decide to figure out what's going on here.

We know that when people become hypercritical, it usually arises out of frustration and having trouble getting what they want. So you respond,

"Darling, I can see that something's not right with you, and you probably feel frustrated, critical, and angry. Let's talk about it." That is an empathic response. You are simply reflecting her feelings.

Sympathy is when you think and feel just like the other person, and in the above example, you might respond, "Darling, you're right. Our neighbor is really no good. He's a sorry SOB, and I don't care if I ever see him again." In this case, you feel exactly like your wife and your response shows you share a mutual dislike of your neighbor. That's sympathy toward your wife.

In the empathy example you are emotionally detached from your wife's feelings—yet still understanding—but in the sympathy example you are as involved as your wife. Thus, a key element of empathy is *emotional detachment*. Looking at several situations that require assertive behavior should clarify these concepts.

In our first example, imagine yourself in a restaurant and you order your steak well done, but when the waitress brings it to you, it is very rare. A *nonassertive* person would most likely go ahead and eat it, saying nothing. An *aggressive* person would likely chastise the waitress angrily with a few choice words for all to hear. Our *assertive* hero might say, "Look, miss, I know you didn't cook this steak, and I can see you're very rushed and busy [*empathy*], but it is rare, not well done like I ordered [*content*], so would you please take it back to the cook [*action*]?"

In our second example, picture your boss as a person who has trouble confronting employees about their poor job behavior. So he handles such situations by sending memos to everyone, which seem to blame everyone for the actions of a few. I call this the "old woman in a shoe" syndrome, spanking all the kids to make sure a few guilty ones get punished. The big problem with such memos is you rarely know to whom they apply. His most recent memo might apply to you, but you're not sure. You decide to speak assertively to him: "Look, Boss, I know you're busy, and dealing with people face-to-face can be tough [*empathy*], but this memo is very confusing. I don't know whether you're addressing me, specific troublemakers, or everyone [*content*]. Therefore, if you ever have a problem with my job performance, call me in so we can talk about it in private [*action*]."

A final example: Your Aunt Bessie calls you all the time and just rambles on and on and bores you with her chatter, rarely talking about anything of substance. Your assertive response is, "Aunt Bessie, I know how important it is for you to call me all the time and talk [*empathy*], but the fact is I simply don't have the time to talk as long as you'd like [*content*], so in the future, we need to keep our conversations short and stick to matters of importance to both of us [*action*]."

I'm sure these examples will give you a feel for assertive responses. And practice will help you even more. The next question is how do you teach your children this skill?

To begin, try not to let them see you acting either non-assertively or aggressively. All your teaching will be for naught if you are not assertive most of the time. Whatever type of behavior they observe coming from you during their formative years is the style of behavior they're likely to adopt.

Next, start off teaching your children how to be *empathic* persons. They can practice on each other and with their friends. Whenever they come in complaining about a playmate's behavior, sit them down and help them analyze it to see why the playmate acts that way. A little girl came to her mother to complain that her girlfriend across the street was acting "mean" toward her—and she didn't know why.

"What did you do?" the mother inquired calmly.

"Nothing," the little girl sobbed. "She just called me names and hit me on the arm."

"Why do you think she did that?" the mother asked.

"I don't know. She's just mean."

"Well, honey, when people act mean toward you—and you didn't do anything to deserve it—it usually means something else is bothering them. Can you think of anything that might be bothering your friend?"

"No," she answered, unable to think beyond her hurt and tears.

"Well, let's see," speculated the mother. "You and I both know that her daddy is in the hospital and is very sick—and might even die! Do you think she might be scared and worried because there's nothing she can do about it, so maybe she's taking her frustration out on you? What do you think?"

The little girl paused and then said tentatively, "Well...maybe."

The mother continued, "Remember when we were at the beach and you were trying to build a sandcastle, but the waves kept washing it away, and your brother laughed at you, so you tried to hit him, but you couldn't because he ran away. Remember how you felt?"

"Yes," she answered.

"Well, just maybe something like that has happened to your playmate because she's in a situation at her house that she can't do anything about. What do you think?"

"Maybe so," the little girl answered.

At that moment, this little girl learned something about empathy, with the guidance of her mother. Opportunities like that will pop up in your children's lives. Make them learning experiences instead of calamities. Then your children will know about empathy.

The next step is to teach the *content* portion of assertive behavior. It's one thing to be able to empathize with others, but it's quite another to know and feel that you have the right to be assertive around others. Many people think that being assertive borders on bad manners, thus they don't have such a right.

The best way to approach this is to get copies of the Declaration of Independence and the United Nations' Universal Declaration of Human Rights. When you read these documents, which are *the* basic outlines of what all our rights as human beings are, you're probably going to be shocked to realize that humankind is very good at figuring out and writing down, in impressive documents, the way life *ought* to be in this world, but we are not very good at putting all this into action.

If you are at all knowledgeable about conditions throughout the world, you will see that there is a big discrepancy between what *ought to be* and *what is*. Most people and nations pay good lip service to the lofty principles in these two documents, but they don't always follow them. But these are the best principles we have, and all the civilized nations have subscribed to those of the United Nations, at least, so you can't go wrong by recommitting to them yourself and teaching your children likewise. And just because many people in the United Nations and in America don't always practice these principles, it in no way demeans or lessens them. They form the bedrock rationale for you to go about life in an assertive manner. And since you cannot always depend on others to secure your rights for you, you need to be prepared to do it yourself when the need arises. Your children will need this skill.

As you study these two documents, you will see that people have a lot of rights. And the only way others can take them from us is if we let them! Assertive people don't let others trample on them. Nor should you or your children. The key is to secure those rights in a socially approved manner.

Thus, the *content* of your assertive behavior rests on the fact that your children have certain rights, which we have boiled down to *request, refusal*, and *correcting wrongs*. You will teach them these rights, and their assertive responses will use these rights as the rationale or reason why they are acting assertively. And if others don't like it at that point—well, that's just too bad! A psychologist friend of mine once said that a little healthy arrogance is good for positive mental health.

The final component of assertive statements is the *action* component. This is simply a summing-up statement of what you want the other person to do, to correct the wrongs that are being done to you.

To sum up, the assertive statement has *empathy* in it, reasonable *content* as to why it's being made, and an *action* component, whereby you're asking the other person to behave in a way consistent with you securing your rights.

In Chapter 6, I related the incident my daughter had with her third grade teacher and how she resolved it. This was an example of assertive behavior, and it quickly developed for her a reputation among the teachers that she was a student with whom they had to be on their toes. Her mother and I never had to intervene in her grade and high school life again, because she developed the ability to handle all questionable situations on her own, though she would usually discuss them with her mother and me before acting. The key point here was that she felt that she had a right to do this.

However, life is not perfect, and even assertive principles need fine-tuning from time to time. After our daughter left for college, she had to deal assertively with poor teachers, sloppy roommates, and the usual problems inherent in college life. As she was finishing her senior year as a mathematics major, she was having trouble with a particular class in theoretical math, which, surprisingly, was proving difficult for her. She was concerned that she might not pass the class and that it would delay her graduation date.

The basic part of the problem was her teacher, from another country, spoke very poor English and could not explain these difficult mathematical concepts clearly. Also, he came from a culture that did not value the role of women as do we in America. She and I discussed the situation, and since she knew that further discussion with the teacher himself would be useless, she decided to go over his head and meet with the dean of the mathematics department. She asked that I go with her as backup, but she was to do most of the asserting. I agreed to the role of the "concerned parent." Besides, I wanted to see how she handled all this and to see her assertiveness in action.

When we walked into the dean's office, it was clear that he and his associate were not used to having students, backed up by parents, confronting them. It was also clear by their servile manner that they didn't want any discord leaking outside their department. Also, we had paid attention to our physical presence, knowing that dress and appearance can be a powerful part in assertion. My daughter and I are very tall people, and we were wearing our conservative, ready-for-business suits. The dean and his assistant were very short men and were casually dressed. I knew as soon as we met them that we had the upper hand.

I sat by quietly while my daughter made her litany of assertive statements about the problems related to the course (which they acknowledged): how difficult it was to get mathematics teachers who understood such complex concepts, how America had a severe shortage of math teachers, how we've had to get our math teachers from foreign countries, how their poor English skills further hamper their abilities to get these difficult math concepts across to the students, the problems it must be causing the university deans, and so on. After giving them all the *empathy* and *content* she could muster, she launched into *action*. She told them that they needed to do something about her situation, and she didn't think that she should suffer unduly because of the university's deficiencies. Sensing victory near, I broke in with my taxpayer spiel (this was a public university) and told them I thought our tax dollars should go to solving this dilemma, such a fine university should have the best teachers, and something needed to be done with both my daughter's situation and the overall problem in general.

After we finished our presentations, they fell all over themselves in conciliatory agreement, thanking us for bringing it to their attention and assuring us something *would* be done. My daughter and I left feeling quite good about the way she handled herself, and we were certain something positive would happen.

However, she got even more than she dreamed. A few days later, she received a letter stating that she was being given credit for successfully completing the course and would graduate on time!

Is this assertiveness stuff powerful, or what?

To sum up, teach your children this simple assertive formula: *empathy*, *content*, and *action*. Model this behavior for your children by your actions. Husbands and wives can do it with each other and let their children watch and learn. If you have more than one child, let the children do it with each other. By the time they are adults they will be experts.

In addition to your training at home, there are activities at your school, church, and community that are fertile assertive-learning situations in which all can participate:

1) Public speaking participation, in which your children talk about their 4-H, scouting, science fair project, or any subject in front of a group

2) Being on a high school debate team

3) Playing on any type of well-coached sports team

4) Participating in a school band or orchestra

5) Giving solo recitals in music, dance, or anything else at which your children are good at doing

6) Acting in school plays

7) Attending family reunions and interacting with others.

You will doubtless think of other activities, but the key is to urge your children to participate in those activities that promote social interaction and require conflict resolution from time to time, enabling them to get their needs met.

If you're parents to whom all this is alien, I suggest you enroll in some assertiveness training courses, which are almost always a part of adult education, extension courses at universities and junior colleges. These are short term and not very demanding, but they will be very helpful to you. Also, check out the many books on this subject in your library or bookstore and on the Internet. For those of you whose non-assertiveness or aggressive behavior is beyond the range of "normal," please get into counseling with a professional counselor who specializes in this area (9).

CHAPTER 9

THE SPIRITUAL DIMENSION

The fact that people need to believe in something beyond themselves and the material world in which they exist is demonstrated by the reality that all major cultures in the world have some sort of religious/afterlife belief system to help them answer that universal question for which our reason and science cannot supply a answer: *What happens to me when I die?* It doesn't matter whether you're Christian, Moslem, Jew, Hindu, Mormon, obscure sect, or whatever; you do your children a disservice if you don't introduce them to a religion (1). And being an agnostic or atheist, and letting them find their own way, or letting them substitute science for religion, often has unpredictable consequences. The best thinkers humankind has produced have been using reason and science in attempts to answer this universal question and have come up empty so far. If the best minds of all time have failed in this attempt, what makes you think you or your children can succeed?

My experience with children is that they want to believe in a higher power and an afterlife. It comforts them and reduces psychological tension when bad things happen to them at an early age and later. All of the major religions give answers to those universal life and death questions—better ideas than you, or I, are likely to dream up. The real world can be extremely harsh and cruel at times, and kids need answers to these onslaughts of life if they are going to keep their equilibrium and develop into successful adults. So don't begrudge your children of this opportunity. And the best way to handle this issue is for the whole family to attend worship services on a regular basis.

A good illustration of the importance of this issue exists in the organization of Alcoholics Anonymous (AA), and all its "spin-off," sister twelve-step programs. When AA was getting a struggling start in the 1930s, most of its founding members were raised in religious households and held varying conceptions of God. And most of them prayed from time to time to their God to relieve them of the awful disease of alcoholism. But their prayers had gone unanswered, so they looked to medicine, psychology, philosophy, education, or any-thing else they could for an answer. But the answer was not forthcoming. Ultimately, they developed what we know today as the Twelve Steps, which is a combination of psychological surrender to the disease, deep self-introspection, acceptance of their misdeeds, retribution to those they have harmed, and service to help other alcoholics. But that wasn't all. Intertwined in all this was the need for a god, or higher power, to whom they had to surrender and submit, so it could help them walk this path of recovery and stay clean and sober. The founders of AA had rediscovered what our ancient forefathers had known: That to effectively deal with many of the major problems in our lives, we have to ground those attempts in a partner-ship with a higher power, or a god, of our under-standing. Without this foundation, we are left only with ourselves—and AA members had proven that didn't work.

AA handled this "god problem" by letting each member define his or her own "god of your under-standing." Some chose the AA organization itself as the "higher power," until they had been sober long enough to develop for themselves a more theologically oriented higher power, or god. This is akin to your young children, who need to have some religious grounding during their formative years, and they can shape and reformulate their religious belief systems as they mature—a lifelong process (2).

Now, I can hear some of you out there already saying that the organized churches around the world are corrupt, misguided, don't practice what they preach, etc. And a lot of this is true. Many wars, terrorist atrocities, and societal perversions have occurred under the aegis of the "church." Some can argue successfully that the church causes more problems than it solves. But when you balance it out and consider what the world would have been like had there been no religious organizations to help us reign in our more basic instincts, one can see that we need our religions. And religion, like everything else, grows and changes, adapting to the times, albeit often too slowly. When thinking about this matter, remember the infamous irreligious people, like Attila the Hun, Adolph Hitler, Joseph Stalin, or Saddam Hussein. Who knows where humankind would be today if people like this had had just a speck of humanity in them as taught by all the major religions.

When your children ask you spiritual questions, tell them what you believe. But let them know that some questions are still unanswered and you and your church are still seeking answers. Tell your children that they should be a part of this quest if they want to be happy. And always assure them that the god of their understanding is good, but still allows bad things to happen, for which there are often no good answers. Two good books that deal with this problem are *When Bad Things Happen to Good People* and *Man's Search for Meaning*. These books will help you better deal with this issue.

The main point here is you want your children to develop religious and philosophic inquiring minds that they will be constantly updating, one that will serve them for an entire lifetime and teach them that it's okay to talk about these issues with like-minded people.

A major part of your responsibility in this area is to help your children associate with other children on a regular basis who have a similar religious belief system. You must protect your children from viewing, on TV and other media, messages that run counter to what you are trying to teach. If you don't take a proactive role here, they will be bombarded with visions and words that may undo what you are trying to teach. And your children must see you associating with like-minded believers and participating in activities that support your beliefs. Faith without deeds to back them up is dead. And, please, do not be one of those parents who trundles the children off to Sunday school on a church bus, while you stay at home and read the Sunday paper.

CHAPTER 10

ALCOHOL AND DRUG USAGE

The world of alcohol and drug usage is a complex one. And children must be taught how to deal with it, or they are at an increased risk of abusing mood-altering chemicals when they are introduced to them by their peers and the society at large—which will happen, whether we like it or not (1).

What parents need to do is teach them a healthy respect for alcohol and drugs, set a good example in their own behavior, and make sure they get the proper information about the various mood-altering drugs as soon as they are capable of assimilating this information.

You do not want to rely totally on others, such as your church, school programs, TV, etc., to get the proper messages across. This is too important and potentially life disturbing to rely too much on others to do this job for you. If your children develop alcohol or drug problems, they will *not* be successful in life. Many people who are addicted can somehow manage to be relatively successful in some areas of their lives, but upon close examination will fall short in other critical areas, such as child rearing, for example. The reason for this is addiction demands considerable time, energy, and money from victims and prevents them from achieving many things in life they otherwise could. A person cannot serve two masters, so take my professional advice: Addiction is a powerful master! Others can augment what you, the parents, can't do, but you must be the main teachers in this area.

So where to begin?

Let's start with alcoholic beverages. Do not—I repeat—*do not* preach "hellfire and damnation" messages about the consumption of alcohol. And why not, you ask? Because that approach is not factual or scientific and has been proven not to work well. Among the more fundamental Christian denominations in America who promote total abstinence, surveys have shown that 40 to 50 percent of these people still drink—and the rate of alcoholism is even higher with them than with those whose religions suggest moderate drinking

(2). This demonstrates how tempting "forbidden fruit" can be to some. It is a fear-based reason not to drink, and for most people who do choose to drink—despite the dire predictions of all the dreadful things that will happen to them—these bad things do *not* happen for 90 percent of these folks. For example, if you preach to your children that drinking alcohol will cause them to suffer some terrible calamity, and later, when they do indulge in alcohol (at the irresistible urging of their peers), and lo and behold, their world does not come to some disastrous end, then you, the wise and all-knowing parents, will have been proven to be people who don't know what they're talking about. Your children will then be less inclined to take you seriously about the other things you preach to them. In fact, the alcohol will make them feel even better for a while, giving them an elated feeling, loosening up their inhibitions, making their peers seem to know more about this than you do—in general making your whole presentation against alcohol look rather stupid. And parents don't need to appear stupid to their children.

Please don't get me wrong here. I am not promoting the usage of alcohol for anyone. I have spent over thirty years counseling alcoholics and have seen the ravages the disease of alcoholism can do to people, and the pictures have not been pretty. The waste of time, energy, productivity, health, and even sanity has been enormous among those who lose control over this chemical. Yes, abstinence has much to commend it, but it should be a personal choice, based on facts—not fiction.

And here are some of the facts on alcohol consumption: Alcohol is a mood-altering chemical that humans have used for thousands of years, going back into prehistory. It was probably the first drug, perhaps discovered by prehistoric people when some rainwater fell into a vat of fruit, fermented, and tasted pretty good, giving all who partook a pleasant buzz. Because alcohol has been a part of our culture so long, it has gained the position of primacy and acceptance. It is ingrained in all of the world's cultures to varying degrees, and this general acceptance has entrenched it so thoroughly that we couldn't dig it out if we wanted to. That great American experiment of Prohibition failed because of this deep cultural entrenchment.

In fact, Christians have no less an authority than Jesus Christ himself promoting the use of alcohol when he changed water into wine at the wedding at Canaan. And later, he chose wine as one of the Sacraments to be used in Holy Communion. So if you try to use Christian teachings to keep your children away from alcohol, you run the risk of confronting the Christ of your children's understanding and sounding somewhat hypocritical. However, Christ, St. Paul, and other Bible people *did* condemn drunkenness, meaning they approved of alcohol in moderation only. As St. Timothy said, "A little wine for thy stomach's sake," again emphasizing moderation. The founder of the Protestant Reformation, Martin Luther, loved his beer and wine but did not abuse it.

Alcohol, like all nonfood, consumable products, has side effects that vary from person to person. And some of these side effects are not good. For reasons not yet totally clear to scientists, about 10 to 20 percent of those who consume alcohol on a regular basis will develop a problem with it. Some of the reasons are hypothesized to be genetic, environmental, mental, or combinations thereof. This is also true of all other mood-altering chemicals, including all prescription drugs (3).

But make no mistake, alcohol is just as dangerous as many illegal drugs. In fact, a high government official, an alcohol and drug rehabilitation physician, told me that if alcohol were discovered today, the fact that such a high percentage of people develop a problem with it would dictate that the U.S. Food and Drug Administration not allow it on the general market, but would approve it for distribution only under controlled prescription procedures (4). So we're not talking about apple pie here.

The problem that parents have is countering all the societal hype and advertisement to which your children will be subjected—from TV light-beer ads promoting the boisterous, sexy, carefree life-style, to wine commercials promoting gourmet living and eating. It's as if one cannot live a fruitful, happy life without these alcohol-infused products. And they're marketed powerfully to our nation's youth. You will note that the hard liquor industry rarely advertises on TV, with the reason being they know they shouldn't push their luck, and to do so might reactivate the prohibitionist movement in this country. (I got this information from a VP of sales with a major liquor distributor.)

So what should you do? First, if you don't drink, tell your children why, at as early an age as possible, when they will be able to understand. You might point out that drinking problems tend to run in families, giving examples in your own family where this has occurred and the problems it caused. You can state that alcohol causes brain damage in some people, especially in those who start drinking at a young age. Drinking has also been shown to "kick" some people over into mental illness, which might not have occurred had they remained abstinent (5). Alcohol also causes birth defects in some newborns, and the American Medical Association and the U.S. Food and Drug Administration recommend that all pregnant women, and those who are trying to get pregnant, totally abstain from alcohol. A little-known fact is men who consume moderate to high amounts of alcohol have less motile sperm, which could possibly cause birth defects. Also, it goes without saying that drinking and driving cause extensive misery in our country through accident fatalities and injuries as well as extensive auto property damage. You might also point out that a high percentage of all homicides and suicides in America are committed when persons are under the influence of alcohol and/or drugs (6).

The bottom line is alcohol is like owning a rattlesnake for a pet. The snake might get used to you if you feed and care for it well, but you never know if it might turn on you and bite. Alcohol is the same. So be careful out there.

So how do you handle things if you choose to drink? The keyword is *moderation*. First, never get drunk yourself, if possible. If you do over-imbibe, don't let your kids see you, then rededicate yourself to responsible drinking. If you can't do this, then you're likely in that 10 to 20 percent we mentioned earlier and you'd better get some professional help.

When you drink at home in front of your kids, never have more than one or two drinks. If social drinking tends to bring out some undesirable aspects of your character, such as argumentative, loud, and boisterous behavior or anger, then don't drink. The message you want your children to get from you when you drink is it really doesn't change Mom or Dad much; at the most, all it does is act as a social lubricant, which makes you a somewhat pleasant person to be around at parties and such.

Several of my Jewish clients have told me that some of their friends drink a bit of wine at evening or main meals, and they give the children very watered-down wine to drink along with the adults, trying to teach the children to copy their parents. And they add that the parents never get drunk on these occasions. The purpose, of course, is to set an example for the children to follow and to teach them how to drink responsibly at an early age. And my experience as an alcohol and drug counselor has proven to me that this is a good technique. It takes the "forbidden fruit" aspect away from drinking alcohol and teaches children the proper lessons. When this technique was used, I never saw an alcoholic come from such a family.

Conversely, I saw a disproportionate number of alcoholics come from families where alcohol was totally forbidden or "preached" against, with the result that many of the young people had a strong desire to try this "forbidden fruit." And because they had been given no guidelines on how to drink, they typically would overdo it and get drunk, time and time again, because it felt so good for a little while. Besides, that's what their friends were doing at those now infamous teen parties in absent-parent homes. And if they had a hangover the next day, so what? That's a small price to pay for so much fun the night before. And, of course, it makes all Mom's and Dad's preaching seem rather ridiculous and old fashioned (7).

So if you have chosen to drink, keep it moderate and under control.

All the other drugs are pretty much the same story. All drugs—including alcohol—are consumed for one reason: *to give the person a mood swing,* so he'll feel even better than when he started, be it relief from pain or just to get "high." It's as simple as that.

All drugs are classified as either legal or illegal, with most of the legal ones under physician/prescription control. You should teach your children to *never* use illegal drugs. And I don't care if half the student body at their school is smoking marijuana, it's an illegal drug and can cause serious problems in young people. The following are some reasons you can use to stress to your children the importance of avoiding illegal drugs:

1) It's against the law, and we obey the law in this family.

2) Almost all illegal drug usage is somehow connected to an undesirable lifestyle.

3) Most of these drugs are very addictive and have drastic negative physical and mental consequences on the human body, and that's why they're illegal!

4) The money that goes into the illegal drug trade promotes all sorts of criminal and immoral behavior around the world.

5) The drug lords and pushers don't pay their fair share of taxes, which means you, the good citizen, have to pay taxes for them to clean up all the personal and societal messes they cause, and in this country it's in the billions and billions of dollars—money we could better spend elsewhere.

These are just a few of the reasons against illegal drug usage, but I'm sure you can think of others.

However, do not get sucked into the "street" logic that tries to justify drug use, such as, "Legalizing drugs is the way to go, and that way the government would be able to collect more tax money and treat those people who develop a problem with it." The correct response to such an argument is, "Yes, son, and there are many well-advised and educated people who argue on both sides of this issue over drug legalization, and I don't know who's exactly right. And, of course, you have a right to your opinion, but I hope you will examine both sides of the issue and then come back to me so we can discuss it further. And if you believe strongly enough about it, why don't you write some letters to our congressmen telling them why you think like you do and see what they have to say about it. Meanwhile, it's unlawful to use illegal drugs, and all members of this family obey the law." I've known a few parents who took this approach with their children, and that was the last they ever heard about the issue.

A little more about marijuana. Many people would have you believe it's harmless. Don't believe it! Marijuana is a lot like alcohol, in that about 80 to 90 percent of the population can use it with little or no major aftereffects. But there are many "pot-heads" out there—people whose whole lifestyle is structured around marijuana. Oh, they can function relatively normally in some cases, but when you talk to them, you get the impression that parts of their brains deserted them forever—especially in the area of dispassionate, critical thinking. And despite what some may say, marijuana—like alcohol—is a gateway drug to more dangerous drugs for some people. And the marijuana of today is much stronger than that used by the hippies of the 1960s. In any event, it's still illegal. Also, recent research has demonstrated quite strongly that marijuana use by young people permanently alters the formation of neurons in the developing brain (8).

With prescription drugs, you must also maintain reasonable caution, and you cannot totally rely on some doctors to be fully informed about the drugs they prescribe. I've had many clients who were addicted to drugs prescribed and monitored by doctors. And you must remember that doctors are primarily educated about the drugs they prescribe by the drug companies' salespeople. And busy doctors often take these salespeople at their word, because they do not have the time to do their own research. Added to the fact that different people react differently to various drugs, it's a hard thing on which to keep a watchful eye. So you must be an informed consumer. You may have noticed that, in recent years, when you get a prescription filled, you also get warnings about potential side effects. Pay attention and report any adverse effects to your physician. Also, there are manuals you can buy that list all legal drugs, so it's a good idea for you to look up any drugs you're taking and note the consequences (9).

I began to get a perspective of this pharmaceutical industry/physician/patient triad problem in the 1970s, when I was assigned a case-load of addicted doctors. Many of them became addicted because they were not aware of the long-term consequences of the drugs they "prescribed" to themselves. When I investigated this problem at two major university medical schools, I saw that physicians' training contained almost nothing on alcohol and very little on the negative consequences of drugs in general. The only doctors who seemed to have a full handle on this problem were those doctors who worked at alcohol and drug rehabilitation centers. The average general-practice doctor out in the community had about twenty drugs he routinely prescribed to his patients, and often had very sketchy information as to how these drugs impacted geriatric patients. All this has improved in recent years, but every patient needs to take responsibility for his or her own drug usage, including over-the-counter drugs.

I'll finish this issue with the story of Betty. She was being treated for alcohol addiction at our clinic. It was 1973. Betty was about forty years old and physically showed the ravages of twenty years of uncontrolled drinking. She had a flushed, ruddy complexion, trembling voice, a little pot-belly, and spindly "bird" legs, often seen in female alcoholics. She came into my office on a Friday afternoon, very agitated and flustered.

"Joe," she began, "I've just figured out that all these emotional problems I'm having have got to be caused by this Valium they're giving me. It's making me nervous and jumpy all the time. I feel like I've got ants in my pants. Can you do something to help me?" she asked desperately.

I scanned her medical records. She was on Valium, a relatively new tranquilizing drug that had been prescribed by the detox physician to calm her nerves. The staff had referred her to me to help her go back to work, but it was clear she was not ready.

"Betty, I don't think you're through with your detox yet. Alcohol withdrawal will cause these symptoms, you know."

"No," she insisted. "I've been sober thirty-two days now, and I've been through detox before and it didn't cause all these feelings. It's this Valium, I tell you. But nobody on the treatment staff will listen to me. Please help me!"

I told her I would talk to the staff at our next patient-planning meeting.

When I brought her situation up a few days later, I was met with mild condescension by the detox physician.

"Joe, the Valium I put her on is exactly what she needs at this time. It will calm her down and has few side effects. She'll be fine."

That was the end of that, because I knew nothing about Valium. Besides, the physician "outranked" me.

I reported this to Betty and she was irate, threatening to leave and go somewhere else, which she did a few days later. I never saw her again.

About two years later, I began to notice that we were getting patients who were being admitted to our clinic for Valium *addiction!* When I talked to the new detox physician, she said that Valium was very addictive and was, in fact, cross-addictive to alcohol, which meant that if you were addicted to one, you were automatically addicted to the other. You could use Valium to substitute for alcohol and detox alcoholics with it. But she did not want to keep them on Valium for more than a few days, because they would get addicted to it, and Valium withdrawal could last about thirty days. So she would prescribe less-addictive tranquilizers if they needed them.

This conversation led me to think back about Betty, and it was clear that she had been right about the Valium, and her detox physician was using a medication on which all the data were not in yet. It took another ten years or so before the medical community became really aware of the addictive dangers of Valium and began to restrict its usage. Meanwhile, we had a slew of Valium addicts, all put on this medication by their friendly physicians (9).

The moral of this story is to teach your children to learn all they can about any medication they take and discuss them thoroughly with their doctors, especially if any problems arise. Also, teach them how to read the labels on over-the-counter medications and follow the directions. To some extent, teach your children how to be their own "physician's assistants."

CHAPTER II

EATING AND EXERCISE

I don't need to tell you that too many Americans are overweight and not in the best physical condition. You can't pick up a newspaper these days without coming across an article lamenting the fact that obesity-related diseases are on the upswing in young and old alike. Coupled with this is our national obsession with dieting—looking for an easy answer to this very serious health problem.

Overweight people are simply not in a position to take advantage of the fact that they'll probably live longer than their parents, thanks to modern medicine, and they are not going to be in the proper physical condition to enjoy this extended lifeline. They are going to be overweight, sedentary couch potatoes, who will become less mobile as they age, unable to participate in many of the physical activities for which they now have the time, and planned for all their lives. And the picture is getting worse, because many of America's children are walking doughboys—fat, out of shape, and setting them up for a sedentary lifestyle at an even earlier age than did their parents.

To lead a vigorous, happy life, one must be in good physical condition, which means eating properly and exercising regularly. And when I say exercise, I mean the kind that makes you breathe hard and sweat. When's the last time you sweated from this kind of exertion?

You can probably remember back to your childhood, when you had to do some hard physical labor, such as pushing a nonmotorized lawnmower, walking a few miles to school, stacking bales of hay in the barn, playing outdoor games, or hoeing a garden. I did all those things from time to time as a child, and remember how hard they were, and how I didn't really want to do most of them any more than I had to. But they were part of my duties or chores and became ingrained as habits, because my parents and other relatives made me do them. Thus, I grew up valuing exercise that led to an end objective, though I still don't like some types of exercise, such as working out with weights or running on a treadmill in a gym—I find that immensely boring. Yet when I play golf, I always walk and carry my clubs or use a pull cart; that type of exercise I enjoy. Most of my golfing friends ride motorized golf carts—and weigh a few more pounds than me. My weight gradually increased about thirty pounds over a thirty-year period when I went from a physically active job to a sedentary office job. But it came back down after I retired and again became more physically active. My eating habits pretty much stayed the same over this period of time. Has your waistline followed a similar pattern?

The task that parents have is to get their children to buy into a lifestyle whereby they'll *like* physical exercise and proper eating. And that's not easy these days. The biggest obstacles to this process are TV, computers, video games, automobiles, hanging out with non-active friends, and of course, the always-present ubiquitous junk foods and drinks. And if your child is bright, and a bookworm, then reading can go on the list as well, though I would not restrict reading due to its many other positive, mind-developing qualities. I became an avid reader around the sixth grade. My mother took note and would sometimes make me lay the book down and go outside to play. Many sedentary actives are beneficial, but parents have to make sure children have a balance and not to overdo them at the expense of exercise.

As soon as your children are old enough, get them outdoors and introduce them to outdoor games. This will condition them to like such activities at an early age. Also, get them to play with other children outdoors. Encourage games where they have to run and frolic. Let them see you engaging in physical activities, such as pushing the lawnmower or raking leaves by hand. Try not to use any more power equipment than absolutely necessary. And please, no riding lawnmowers! All these machines do is give children the impression that this is exercise, which it isn't. Sitting your fanny behind the steering wheel of a motorized machine and riding all over the landscape is not the kind of exercise we're looking for. The exercise has to be vigorous enough to get your heart pumping fast (1). One lady told me that her son got plenty of exercise because he was always on the go, driving his car, selling products, and visiting his friends. She really believed this was exercise! So let your kids see you sweat—both Mom and Dad.

Tell your children that recess (if your school still has it), physical education, and sports at school are just important as their academic subjects. Encourage them to participate in those athletics at school that suit their interests and abilities. Keep this emphasis up all through their school years. Depending on their personalities and abilities, they'll come to feel positively about physical exercise by engaging in these activities.

And don't forget to assign them occasional hardworking, sweating chores from time to time. But be sure to reward them for the successful completion of these tasks. A hard task, followed by a desired reward, conditions children to want to repeat the task for further rewards, eventually leading to an important attitude shift, whereby the task itself becomes pleasurable, in and of itself, and further reward will not be needed.

It's no secret that America has more than its share of couch potatoes. A friend of mine recently returned from an extensive trip to Europe, and he reported that Europeans can tell Americans from the natives by simply noting our obesity. "They can see us coming down the street," he reports (2).

Thus, it's clear we eat too much, as well as not exercising enough. Whereas people used to *eat to live*, we now *live to eat*! Dining out is one of Americans' favorite pastimes. Cookbooks are among the most popular literary genre, leading just about every other category of books in sales. There are food networks on TV that have nothing but food-related programs, and regular TV devotes extensive time to cooking shows and demonstrations (3). I don't know what the percentage of advertising is on TV and in other media promoting food products, but it's high, especially that which is targeted at children.

Almost all of our social functions are inexorably tied to food: church bake sales, family reunions, Super Bowl parties, business lunches, picnics, etc. In my town, we have concerts in the park where people bring picnic baskets, eating and listening to the music. In my church, between the services, you can enjoy coffee, donuts, cakes, bagels and cream cheese, cookies, lemonade, and other high-calorie, tasty treats. Typically, all the sponsors of our new church members are served a full breakfast in appreciation of all their "hard" work. A simple thank-you doesn't seem to be enough!

Now, it would be impossible for us not to do these things to some degree; after all, we are sociable people, and we do have to eat. But it is possible to enjoy an activity without food. A simple lesson here for you and your children is *not* to reward them with food. Keep the food confined to sit-down mealtimes as much as possible.

You may think I'm belaboring this issue, but it's obvious we've gone a bit too far, as our excess pounds and obesity-related diseases will testify. The American airline industry says that the average American gained ten pounds during the 1990s, and this extra weight translated to 350 million extra gallons of jet fuel used, at a cost of $27.5

million per year. No wonder airline tickets cost so much!

On top of all this social eating is the fact that we consume too much of the wrong kinds of foods, mainly carbohydrates and fats. This is no secret to you diet-conscious readers. The issue is what can you do about it as you raise your children?

Again, it's no secret that most eating habits are established by what you do at home—what you serve your children and how much. Do you allow extensive snacking, and on what kinds of foods? Does your family eat lots of pizzas, hamburgers, hot dogs, french fries, cakes, cookies, chips, candies, soft drinks, etc.? Do you eat out often at fast-food eateries, with their high-carb, fatty meals and sugary drinks? Does your family consume soft drinks instead of water or skim milk? Is your refrigerator full of soft drinks?

You know the drill here. The food industry panders mostly to our weak side, pushing sweet-tasting snacks and those satisfying "comfort" foods that are loaded with fats, rather than offering what is best for you and your children nutritionally. The empty calories abound in our plates and our lives. But we shouldn't totally blame the food industry; after all, they're simply giving us what we want. And the production of food *is* a business.

While consumers have to share some of the blame for those pants that no longer fit, or for their recent diagnoses of diabetes, the food industry's advertising of their products is so sophisticated that most of us have come to regard such foods as basic staples, which have become integrated into our nation's psyches and our individual personalities. Do you remember all the hoopla over "New Coke" a few years ago? You would have thought that the nation's drinking water supply had been cut off. And all over some sugared, flavored fizz water!

So what should you do? If you don't already know, then learn which are the best foods. The information's out there, so go find it and use it. Then start preparing and serving these foods to the whole family. Start when your children are still in the crib. Mothers should breast-feed their children as long as possible. Let your children grow up eating fruits, vegetables, nuts, skim milk, whole grains, etc. Don't keep cakes, cookies, soft drinks, and candies around the house.

Don't let your children watch TV shows whose sponsors are the purveyors of these substandard foods. You already know how powerful TV ads are, and they can easily override all your efforts if you're not careful.

When your children start school, don't let them eat cafeteria food until you have checked it out. Most school cafeteria food consists of pizza, hamburgers, hot dogs, french fries, and the like, with nutritional value just a bit more than cardboard. What good foods they do serve are usually bypassed by the kids. Instead, fix them one of your special high-nutrition lunches to take with them each day. And teach them how to handle any teasing or ridicule they might get from their peers about not eating what the rest of the herd is grazing on. One helpful technique is for everyone in the family to take his or her own nutritious lunches to school and work. I remember my dad taking his lunch in a black lunchbox with a thermos. I couldn't wait to do the same at school. I probably ate in the school cafeteria less than a dozen times in twelve years.

Next, teach your children how to cook—boys as well as girls! If you've got some macho thing that says kitchens are for girls only, forget it and get into the twenty-first century! You cannot predict that your boy will marry a cute little homemaker who is well versed in the culinary arts and will feed your precious offspring for the rest of his life, negating the need for him to learn how to cook. Those days are pretty much gone in America, what with most women working outside the home, with the husband and wife sharing the household duties. In fact, nowadays, most households are eating out a high percentage of time instead of preparing meals at home. Eating out has three strikes against it: It's expensive, high in fat and carbs, and the portions are too large. This is a major contributor to obesity.

The basics of cooking are not difficult. If your children know how to read and follow instructions—which you and the school system have dutifully taught them—then they can prepare a meal from a cookbook. My wife felt so strongly about teaching children to cook that she and her partner wrote and published a microwave cookbook for kids that was a great success. She found that most kids like learning to cook, because it's an adult thing to do, and those skills will last them a lifetime (4). So teach them the basics of cooking.

And here's a little side effect of boys not cooking that most have never thought of: Suppose your son marries, lives to a ripe old age, but doesn't know how to cook because you didn't teach him; thus he has relied on his wife's cooking all those years—and she dies first. Get the picture? What do you think is going to happen? One of two things: He'll probably start eating out a lot or eating pork and beans out of cans, or he'll rush into another marriage with the friendly widow down the street, just to get a cook and a maid. Think this can't happen? Believe me, it can. I've seen it happen so many times over the years that I can usually predict the next occurrence. Not that there's anything "wrong" with such marriages, because they also provide companionship to the partners involved, but being hungry is not a good motivation for marriage, but I guess hunger can sometimes seem like love! Additionally, such marriages can also cause problems in the rest of the family.

In summary, weight control is a balanced act between physical activity and eating. Children who are on the move constantly are going to be healthy, hungry children who will most often eat whatever you put in front of them. If they are not overindulged with unhealthy, between-meal snacks, they won't be overweight and will not be subject to that most odious of childhood experiences—namely, teasing from schoolmates for being fat! Childhood obesity can set up a lifelong psychological pattern of negative feelings and self-image in response to such teasing, and all your reassurances to the contrary won't amount to much at all. And most childhood-onset diabetes results from eating too much of the wrong foods and not getting enough exercise

So introduce, participate in, and reinforce good eating habits and physical exercise. And please don't make them clean those plates because of all the starving children in Third World countries!

CHAPTER 12

SEX AND MARRIAGE

There's a funny thing about our society and the way we handle sex education with our children. Most parents basically handle it by not dealing with it at all! They simply don't talk about sex, letting their children find out about it from their friends, the media, or other sources. That's not to say that children can't learn about sex from outside sources, such as relatives, teachers, church programs, observing animal behavior, literature, and the like. In fact, whether you like it or not, your children are going to get sex information from these and other sources, and most children handle this well and fairly realistically.

But at some point, you should talk to your children about sex and what it means. And you should do this when your children are ready for such information, which you will have to determine by observing their behavior and then deciding whether they will be able to understand your teachings. I call this "sex readiness," and children vary enormously as to when they are ready for it. In general, the ages of six to ten seem to fit most children. Your children will usually let you know by asking questions (1).

One parent decided that his eight-year-old daughter was ready for his wisdom on this matter, so he proceeded to explain, in clinical detail, the procedures of the sex act and how men and women performed sex both for pleasure and to produce children. When he was finished, the daughter looked at him in disdain and said, "Dad, that's disgusting!" She wanted no part of it at that time, and it was clear that he had introduced her to more than she was ready for.

So, all you enlightened parents out there don't be in such a hurry to drag your children into the ways of adults. But do keep a sharp eye open as to when they'll need this information. They will usually give you some clue as to when they want more information—like the young boy who saw two dogs copulating and asked his father what they were doing. The father took this cue and explained the sex act to the boy, emphasizing that was the way all animals did it, including his mother and father. The kid looked at the father and said, "Oh..." and asked no more questions. That was all he wanted to know at that time.

The biggest part of the problem between children and parents discussing sex is embarrassment. It's just a subject that's hard to talk about in our culture, especially the intimate details. Parents may have some hang-ups themselves, or children simply may not want to talk about such things with their parents. But the information should be given, and this is an area where a good book about sex can be helpful. My mother's deceased father was a physician, and she had many of his medical books in our home, and I would occasionally pull one out and look at the illustrations, which were quite graphic. So I had a good idea about sex at a fairly young age. But I really wasn't all that interested then; sex certainly wasn't as compelling as baseball or my comic books!

If you and your children are the types who can deal with this subject in a frank, open manner, then go to it.

At this point, I want to make as strong a statement as possible about parents' responsibility to protect their children from pornography, sexual perversions, and sexual abuse. There is no place for any of this in children's lives—or that of adults either for that matter. But we all know this deviance is rampant, not only in our society, but around the world. Internet porn is rampant, and many people defend it under the "freedom of the press" rubric. There are sexual predators out there and they'll get your children if they can. In all my years of working with mentally ill clients, about 60 to 80 percent of my female mentally ill or addicted clients had been abused sexually by adult males (2). These abusers were usually stepfathers, uncles, church workers, teachers, or neighbors—people they knew! In fact, of those women who came to me with a diagnosis of multiple personality disorder (now called dissociative disorder), every one of them had been sexually and/or physically abused as young girls. And many of my gay clients were introduced to homosexual abuse as children by older children or adults, usually under the guise that it was "okay" behavior. And these homosexual clients whom I saw had serious emotional problems as well.

Here's how all this plays out in the life of children: When children are abused sexually, the abusers usually keep the children silent by threatening harm to them, or by threatening to hurt their parents. Of course, no young children want harm to come to them or their parents, so they usually keep quiet. But the children know that what has occurred is not right, so they have to construct, with their childlike minds, some rationale or justification for keeping quiet and not reporting the abuse. This is then the beginning of their departure from reality and possible entry into the beginnings of serious emotional problems or mental illness. Compounding this process is the fact that, in some cases, the sexual abuse may be pleasurable to children, and this usually leads to an enormous buildup of guilt, which of course also has to be covered up. Later, they may take up deviant behavior, such as smoking or alcohol and drug abuse, to help numb the pain. Or they may, like my clever, flamboyant client, Alice, develop fifteen different personalities, into which they escape to avoid the awful truth, long after the abuse has stopped (3).

Another terrible thing that occurs with such abused children is, for some reason, they usually develop the idea that the abuse is their fault, and that they are bad children and deserve this punishment. And, of course, they're not going to tell this to anyone. Child abusers somehow know about these propensities of their victims to remain silent about the abuse, so they cleverly use it to get to continue their despicable behavior (4).

What should you, the parents, do? Make it your business to know whom your children are with at all times. Learn all you can about the people they are with when you're not around, which includes teachers, church workers, scout leaders, neighbors, relatives, playmates, or anyone with whom your children are occasionally alone. Next, talk to your children in a nonthreatening way, asking them to report to you if anyone ever "touches" or hurts their genital area. I think it best if the mothers talk to the girls about this and the fathers talk to the boys.

A final thing about sexual predators: Many of them seek employment in jobs that put them in daily contact with children. So keep an alert, discerning eye in this regard.

I once had a client who was introduced to homosexual activity at age twelve by a cousin. He said that the activities were confusing to him at the time, but were pleasurable, so he allowed the abuse to continue. Besides, he had no mother or father at home, only an elderly grandmother, who he didn't think would understand. He said his cousin would "beat him up" if he told anyone.

Thus, his homosexual activity continued out of habit and opportunity on through high school. There was an occasional sexual encounter with a female, but he reported that those episodes felt strange to him, so he usually "stayed" with the boys. So my client entered adulthood as pretty much a homosexual, liking younger boys and acting on his desires. Eventually, he was caught, tried, and prosecuted, put on probation, and wound up in my office for counseling and job assistance.

His probation officer and I developed a plan consisting of therapy, counseling, job placement, and payment of his court fines. However, he was not allowed by the court to get a job working around children. After much effort, we succeeded in getting him a job as a kitchen worker in a restaurant, with his boss promising him a better job as a waiter if he performed his duties satisfactorily for four months.

The client eagerly began his new job, but when I called him two weeks later, he said he had left that job and got a better one.

"What would that be?" I inquired suspiciously.

"I'm working at the XYZ Day Care Center, taking care of children," he announced matter-of-factly.

I was astounded. He was totally disconnected to the reality of his situation. A quick phone call to his probation officer and it was back to jail for him. Some people really don't learn well. And child abusers are among them.

Relating properly to the opposite sex is a critical skill, and everyone needs to learn how to do it effectively. Whether it's an opposite-sex boss, a spouse, a child, a relative, a date, or a friend, we all need to know how to handle the "oppositeness" that comes from the fact that there are two sexes, with different hormones coursing through our veins.

The biggest problems seem to start in the teen years, with the pursuit of the dating game. Everyone is familiar with the awkwardness of adolescence, which, if not handled well, can develop some lifelong hang-ups. Modern sociologists say that adolescence now extends to age thirty! The basic reason for this is we have to adapt to a more complex world and it now takes longer to get an adequate education. There is some recent research that says the social-learning areas of our brains don't stop growing until about the age of twenty-five, which might explain much of the goofy behavior we see in college students and others in this age bracket.

Social demands on an individual are more complicated than they used to be. Modern, complex social behavior now takes longer to learn (hence books like this). Greater sexual freedom for young people, thanks to modern birth control, has given our youth more freedom—with more opportunities to manage their sex lives poorly. And it just takes longer for them to position themselves where they need to be.

Before the early 1900s there was no such thing as adolescence. In the America of the nineteenth century, you were most likely raised on a farm or in a small town, and you could get a good job without much education, as long as you were industrious, healthy, and hardworking. Thus, most young people would drop out of school as soon as they reached puberty, get a job, get married, and go on about their lives.

But we can't do that anymore. If a girl drops out of school, gets married, or starts having children outside of marriage, she will pretty much doom herself to a lifetime of very hard struggle and poverty. You just can't do it the old-fashioned way anymore.

Which brings about the dilemma that a teenager must struggle with: "If I'm reaching puberty at a young age, and I'm now sexually ready to go, and you people tell me that I must hold off until I'm educated and economically ready for marriage, then what am I supposed to do with all these sexual urges that are tormenting me? Wait 'til age thirty? Get real!"

All parents should help their children with this issue by at least talking about the impossibility of it. But almost none do, because they don't know how. All most of us parents know is the imperfect way we handled it, the messes we made, and how we don't want our kids to have to go through the same business.

So what's the answer? There has to one somewhere, doesn't there? After all, children now have all these new venereal diseases to deal with, diseases that were rare or nonexistent when we were growing up. The sexual diseases of the 1940s and 1950s could be cured with antibiotics, right? But not anymore. At least not herpes and AIDS.

The sad thing is your children are going to have to go through this period of their lives struggling with most of the same issues that you did. And you have to instill in them that in the affairs of sex and love they're going to have to use plenty of common sense, put their head in charge of their sexuality, and be very, very careful.

Common sense then dictates that children have to learn to relate effectively to the opposite sex as early as possible, and to the extent that they are developmentally ready. Boys should be taught that they are *never, ever* to hit a girl— period! Teach them about sex as soon as they show interest. Let young people mix in various social situations—always under some sort of adult supervision—teaching them the rules of conduct. When they start dating, establish *your* rules of conduct. Also, the parents should set the age when the children can start dating. My experience with clients suggests that sixteen is a good age. I have seen too many children, ages six to early teens, who are already in the dating game, pushed by their parents or peers long before they were even interested on their own. Parents who allow this have usually gotten a distorted idea that sooner is better. Parents, let your children be children as long as they want to be. What's the big rush?

Now, the birth control issue is a touchy one, with which parents have to deal. All sorts of birth control measures are available to everyone, such as condoms, birth control pills, contraceptive foams, various mechanical devices, and the old rhythm method. What most parents desire is for their children to abstain from all sex until they get married. And some follow this choice—but not the majority.

Sex among the unmarried is now the norm, as evidenced by all the children being produced by single women. Up until the 1960s, unmarried, pregnant girls were chastised by their communities and were hustled off to special homes until the birth of the baby, which was promptly offered up for adoption. This was pretty harsh, but it inhibited most girls from getting pregnant until they were married. Of course, the burden of control on all this was placed mostly on the woman—not the man!

But now that has all changed. The stigma is now mostly gone and our society rewards unwed mothers with financial welfare benefits.

So parents should discuss all these factors with their children at the time they deem proper, and recognize that despite their best efforts they may still behave in ways that are disliked, but keep up the hope that any sexual activity does not lead to a compromised life. That's the best a parent can do.

Regarding marriage, as we all are well aware, this institution is being eroded. Over 50 percent of all marriages in America end up in divorce. I don't know whether cavemen "married" their mates or not, but from recorded history we can see that men and women tended to bond to one mate—with a little bit of fooling around on the side! An old sociology professor of mine said that, in ancient times, it was one man bonded to one woman, because that was the only way they could determine who the property went to when they died (6)! And in the prehistoric days, property or possessions were more important than they are today.

Some Mormons, Middle Easterners, and others may have many wives, but that's not without its problems. In his book *Roughing It*, Mark Twain documented the problems that Brigham Young had with his many wives and children, enough to make one think that one wife or husband is enough!

So it's unclear whether humans as a species are genetically monogamous or not. Canadian geese are monogamous, as are porpoises, robins, cardinals, and countless other animals. But apes aren't. Neither are chimpanzees, dogs, cats, and probably the majority of all animals. It is possible that humankind is predisposed to many sexual partners, especially when we examine the sex lives of those celebrities who aren't smart enough to keep things undercover, so to speak.

It's my experience that, among the thousands of clients whom I've had over the years, fidelity is the *exception* rather than the *rule*. It seems most people cannot stay sexually faithful to their partners all the time. But of all the people who *were* 100 percent faithful to their spouses, *all* were psychologically well-adjusted people. Now, they might get the idea, like President Carter admitted in a *Playboy* magazine interview, to stray and sin in their own minds on occasion, but they didn't follow those thoughts with adulterous behavior.

So I'm going to propose a position here with which you may or may not agree. I'm advising you to promote in your children the ideal of *no sex before marriage, and once you get married, no fooling around*. And the most powerful way for you to do this is for your children to watch you be faithful to your spouse, then they'll know that Mom and Dad practice what they preach. This strategy won't work if one commits adultery and trys to excuse it with, "I'm a sinner and weak. I'll never do it again. God will forgive me. Why can't you?" This is a leaky bucket at best, and your spouse and children can see through it as if your soul were made of cellophane. They know that words are becoming increasingly cheap in this day of hype and spin. Behavior is what counts.

Now, some young people will tell you that "shacking up," or living together before marriage, is the rational thing to do, because it's a test run to see if two people are compatible sexually, emotionally, and in other ways. They will tell you that this is becoming the way of life in Europe, especially Scandinavian countries. However, the institution of marriage is dying in Europe, due to several factors, such that the statistics on marriage and divorce from Europe are now useless (5).

I contend that there's a good case to be made for a long courtship and engagement period, with no sexual intercourse before marriage, and this will promote the following:

1) It sets a good example for your own children, in that you can promote it with a clear

conscience and an un-twitching eye and not be a hypocrite.

2) It will make the honeymoon more unique and fun, setting up good memories that will last a lifetime.

3) It will absolutely prevent the necessity for "shotgun" weddings.

4) It will prevent the spread of various venereal diseases.

5) It will force the young couple to struggle with their own emotionality regarding sex, which will strengthen them in ways in which they are likely to be unaware.

6) It will prevent gossip and snide remarks that always arise in the minds of some people.

7) It fits in beautifully with the Christian, Jewish, Moslem, and other religious traditions about marriage and sex. It's unclear how hedonists, agnostics, and atheists will view this.

8) It will prevent inappropriate emotional entanglements among young people and keep them from falling into dysfunctional relationships they never anticipated.

There are other reasons I'm sure you can think of, but the most powerful one is that sex can be approached in two fundamental ways: As an impersonal, unemotional act, such as paying for sex from a prostitute; or as a deeply personal, emotional union, signifying that a relationship in marriage is unlike any other in life and should not be trivialized by casualness and infidelity.

In conclusion, a successful marriage is one where the couple stays married and works out their inevitable differences. They do not cut and run without there being catastrophic reasons. Research has shown, and my experience as a counselor has affirmed, that a married couple who can express their negative and positive feelings to each other in an assertive manner when the need arises will ultimately be able to work things out and remain married. If your children see you doing this, they are likely to follow suit as adults. Conversely, couples who can't express their feelings to each other, who talk around emotional issues and rarely deal with them—other than to get angry with one another—are sooner or later very likely heading for divorce court (6).

A final piece of advice here: After all I've said—even if you repeat similar advice to your children—the fact is there's a great chance they're still going to engage in sex before marriage anyway. Those hormones are flowing and you can't cut them off with your words and protestations. So about the best you can do—in addition to the above suggestions—is to say something like, "Look, I know abstinence from sexual intercourse is hard, but if you do decide to do it, please take the necessary precautions so as not to produce children outside of marriage."

CHAPTER 13

WORK AND LEISURE

While it is important to teach your children how to work hard when necessary, it is just as critical to teach them how and when to rest and have fun. I once had a client who had a brutally hard working life as a child on the farm, and he was the hardest-working teenager in his area. The problem was his father didn't let him learn to use what leisure time he had to have fun, so the young man left the farm as soon as he completed high school, joined the Army, and spent the next twenty years not doing much of anything. After retiring from Army life, he opened a country store, and about all he did was sit around the store all day and talk with customers about the weather and such. On meeting him in person, you had the feeling that he was the laziest man alive. Most of his adult life was spent in overreaction against his hard life as a child. This is not the way to go about a career.

Since we live in a work-oriented society, whereby we earn the money to purchase the "tools" necessary to meet our needs and become happy people, children need to learn about work and its proper role in their lives. In his book *Jobs of the Future*, Marvin Cetron says, "Working means money, a home, a car, vacations, entertainment, education for the kids, and a secure retirement (1)." I would add adequate health care, financing for leisure activities, food, and life's other incidental expenses.

Psychiatrist Dr. William Menniger states that work is psychologically important because it is one of the most useful outlets for hostility and aggression; it's also where we can win approval from others for what we do, and it helps us develop satisfying social relationships (2).

So there's no question that work is important. If you aren't convinced, try hanging around those who are unemployed and can't find jobs. They will most likely be very unhappy and depressed people.

Start your children out by talking about your work in a positive manner. Let your children know what you do when you go to work. When your children are old enough, take them to work with you so they can see firsthand what you do. If you are a stay-at-home parent, let your children know that your ordinary household duties are work, even though you don't get paid for them.

The first place children usually learn about work is through the performance of chores, such as cleaning up their rooms, washing dishes, taking out the garbage, or mowing the lawn. The reward is twofold: An allowance is tied to performance of the chores, and they get social approval from the parents. Your children may resist doing chores from time to time, in an effort to establish their own free will and individual initiative. However, it is important that you teach them that there will be no allowance until the chores are completed. And if withholding the allowance doesn't work, some sort of punishment will be in order, usually by withholding a much-desired privilege. The major lesson to be learned here is if they complete their chores, they will get the allowance to buy those things they like and will receive your social approval.

This process is where good attitudes toward work begin. Over time, this will become a habit in your children and it will develop it into a sense of self-responsibility, which they will always want to do. Later, your children will feel uncomfortable if they *don't* do their work, and it's this uncomfortable feeling that you want to instill in your children.

This *subconscious feeling* will then become a main motivator for working, and it's the main reason why unemployed people are not happy campers. The only way to make this unpleasant feeling go away is to go to work!

Later, school and its requirements of academic work will reinforce what you've already begun, and your children should then develop into hard-working, studious, achieving children in the school system.

But there's one critical thing to watch out for in the school situation: Often, there will be a group of students in the school who have not yet learned this process, and as a result, they may be those classic underachievers we're always hearing about. And they will try to pass on their underachieving philosophy to all who will join their group. These are kids who have never learned to take on responsibility or what work is all about. Since there's safety in numbers, they try to "recruit" others to join them in their lazy ways, under the subconscious premise that if they have enough like-minded people around them, then they must be right, and all those hardworking nerds are wrong. This is one way teenage gangs get started.

So, do what you must to get your children associated with the "hardworking" crowd in school, so they will reinforce what you've been trying to develop in your children at home. This is not hard to do—simply monitor and control what type of kids your children hang around with.

All this being said, you do not want to create workaholics of your children, something that is, incidentally, hard to do anyway. You do not want to produce a Type A, driven, obsessive, workaholic personality types who can never seem to relax and have fun. You know the saying, "All work and no play makes Jack a dull boy." Well, it's the truth, and the Jacks of the world are very prone to all sorts of stress-related illnesses as they age (3).

Avoid this problem simply by rewarding your children with "fun things" after they complete their chores or schoolwork. Don't reward them only with money, because that will tend to make them too money conscious, perhaps inclining them to work too much. Instead, reward them with "time-out" periods, whereby they can do whatever they want. Teach them about vacations by doing something together as a family, and let them know that the vacation is a reward for the whole family for all the hard work they do in their various jobs. Many parents do not understand that time spent with the parents is usually a reward to the children, so use yourself as the great reward!

When our children were ages nine and twelve, my wife had an important business trip to the

National Booksellers Convention in San Francisco. She and I decided it would be an excellent opportunity for the rest of the family to accompany her, so we could better learn about her work (which was to sell the cookbooks that she had written and published) and reward us all for hard work well done. Even though it was the middle of the school year, we pulled the kids out of class, and I took a week of leave from my job. We told the children that the trip was a reward for all their good work at school, doing their chores, and for just being good kids.

We had a wonderful trip. It was the children's first airplane trip, with a wonderful visit seeing the sights of San Francisco. The kids roamed the huge convention floor freely, visiting hundreds of the booksellers' booths, meeting people from all over America. They got to meet many celebrities who were there promoting their books, and they got many free books, some autographed, which we shipped ahead back home.

When the convention was over, we rented a car and drove around the city, crossed the Golden Gate Bridge, saw the redwoods, visited the Napa Valley Wine Country, and then drove south and traveled the length of the Big Sur highway, marveling at the many areas where the scenic west coast of California met the boiling Pacific Ocean in explosions of rocky landfalls. We visited Carmel and the Pebble Beach area and spent a night in a state park motel, seeing more giant redwoods. We traveled on farther south until we came to the Hearst Castle at San Simeon, then crossed over the foothills and headed back north up through the Salinas Valley, right through the heart of California's agricultural country. A visit to an old Spanish mission was a highlight.

This trip indelibly imprinted in our children that hard work is followed by fun, rest, and relaxation. And when they got back to school, they worked even more studiously, proving that old psychological maxim that the way to increase certain behaviors are to reward them (4).

So we can see that the development of good work habits and the constructive use of leisure time go together quite well. Again, the most powerful tool in this process is the example set by the parents. If you're a lazy parent who lies around and doesn't work, then all your lectures to your children are nothing more than an empty breeze. But if your children see you going off to work every day, or doing your daily house and yard work, then you're on the right track. Assigning your children their chores will then let them copy your behavior. Also, stress that their schoolwork is also their job, and they are expected to do it just like you do yours. At the same time, emphasize that their hard work will be followed by rest, fun, and relaxation.

If your family attends church try to make Sunday and other religious days fun. Make them a family affair; everyone attends together, sees friends, and is perhaps followed by visits to the zoo, a movie, a ball game, or eating out.

One of my father's favorite gambits was to say he'd take me to our local small-town baseball games in the evenings if I had my chores completed and my homework done. This was especially rewarding to me because, aside from my compulsive interest in baseball, the cool evenings were a welcome respite from the daytime summer heat in Florida. Hunting and fishing trips or visits to the beach were also understood by me to be rewards for doing what I was supposed to do. My parents knew what activities I loved, so they made them the rewards for doing my chores and schoolwork. Gradually, I began to enjoy my assigned duties, because I knew they would be followed by great rewards.

Conversely, too much leisure time without work only leads to slovenliness, lethargy, and poor character development. Probably the most famous example in our society today is the "welfare mom" who sits around all day, doing not much more than minimal household chores, watching too much TV, and gradually getting more depressed and angry about her position in life. She usually has like-minded friends, lives in government housing, is often overweight, and lacks the energy to teach her kids the lessons we're discussing here.

While some readers may think I'm over generalizing, believe me, I'm not. There are plenty of folks who fit the above description. I know because I've had hundreds of them on my caseload over the years. Also in 1960, in the Washington, DC area, I was a census worker who was sent into those areas of town where many people of this type lived, to "enumerate," or count them. Most of them were single, female parents, who impressed me with being somewhat overwhelmed with their lives, having too many children to adequately tend to alone—definitely not happy people. And this was before the Great Society programs were enacted! Thirty years later, as a vocational rehabilitation counselor, the state welfare agency asked me to work with a certain female client to see if I could help her go to work. She was about fifty years old and had never worked at a paying job. When her records arrived, I was flabbergasted to see that she had given birth to eleven children by ten different men or thereabouts—she wasn't quite sure! You never saw a more worn out, depressed, overweight, lethargic person in your life. Needless to say, despite extensive efforts on my and other professionals' parts for over two years, we were unsuccessful in helping her go to work!

What do you think children from such environments learn from situations of this type? I've had many of such children later as adult clients, and they were usually confused, addicted, mixed-up people who wasted years trying to learn what they have to do in life to succeed. Most of them never learned.

Getting more job-specific, the U.S. Department of Labor classifies almost all jobs available in America—that's their function. When I last checked, there were over seventy thousand different jobs available for your children to choose from whenever they're ready to go to work. That's a lot of jobs! In fact, it's overwhelming! What if you were a kid who walked into a candy store with seventy thousand different candies to choose from, but had only enough money to buy one item. That would be a difficult decision.

Careers are like that, but most people don't think about it that way. In fact, most people are familiar with about ten to twenty jobs at the most, and that's what they usually pick from. They most often take whatever job they can get without giving it much thought at all. They learn about a few jobs from what they see in the movies and on TV, or what their immediate circle of family or friends do for a living. They usually know about police officers, firefighters, doctors, lawyers, nurses, dentists, cabdrivers, truckers, professional sports figures, farmers, sales clerks, etc. But even then, they only know the surface details about these jobs, usually only those aspects that have been glorified and presented by the media.

And when kids get out of high school, they have just enough information about these jobs to be dangerous career selectors. So they pick a job based on what they saw on TV, and later find out it was nothing like what they thought it would be. For example, a young person decides to become a teacher because he wants to help young people learn, based on being exposed to teachers all his young life, only to find out later that what he saw his teachers do was just part of the picture. He then learns that the job requires he become a disciplinarian and paper shuffler, having to attend endless meetings and planning sessions. Or a girl becomes a social worker to help the underprivileged, only to find out that the bureaucracy in which she works is stifling and unresponsive, that the clients are unmotivated to improve their lives, and she can't make enough money. A young man joins the Navy to learn to work on aircraft, only to find out that advancement and pay are poor, often working with people of questionable motivation to even be in military service, having to endure boring military rituals, and he's held in low esteem by the general public—unless there's a popular war going on!

So how do you help your children avoid these pitfalls? First, make sure they get a good fundamental education (as we discussed in Chapter 4). Next, expose them to as many vocations as possible during their childhood. And don't sugarcoat the jobs; let them see them warts and all! When they get into high school, encourage them to get to know their school guidance counselor, but please be aware that this counselor is probably not going to be able to help your children with the fundamental problem of what they want to be when they grow up, the reason being that these high school counselors have too many students to shepherd. So about all they're going to be able to do with your children is hit the high spots. Some schools may be worse and some better than the above scenario, so you will have to plan accordingly.

One thing to watch for, however, is the fact that teenagers' interest patterns can bounce all over the place. One week they want to be doctors, and the next, rock stars. The way to handle this is to encourage them to explore many different careers, find out the amount of money they can expect to earn, and determine what the actual everyday job duties will be (5).

Next, help them go beyond their *interests* and look at their *abilities*. And there's a good reason to focus on abilities, because people are usually happiest doing those things they're good at. If your son is not super coordinated athletically, he will not be able to make it as a professional baseball player. If your daughter has proven that she's not good at chemistry and biology, and has a poor academic record, she's not going to make it as a doctor. If your son is not strong in math and physics, engineering is not the field for him. Conversely, if your son is a whiz at taking machines apart and putting them back together, then the field of mechanics might be his thing to pursue (6).

We discover our abilities in three main ways. First, they tend to run in families because they are often inherited. Second, as your children mature, they discover certain abilities through schooling and trying things out. Children are great experimenters and it doesn't take them long to discover what they're good at or can learn to be good at. Third, they can take vocational tests that will point out their various abilities.

However, please be aware that all abilities are not necessarily innate, or determined at birth by your DNA, but are enhanced by interests and practice. Some children can become quite skilled in an endeavor in which they may have only average ability, simply by engaging in enormous amounts of repetitive practice. For example, as a child, when I first started playing baseball, I was an average hitter at best. But something about baseball so appealed to me that I decided to practice and get better. So I devised a practice regimen whereby I would toss small pebbles into the air and hit them with a broomstick. I did this for countless hours and got so good at it that, at one point, I hit over a hundred in a row without missing. As a result, I became one of the best hitters in my league. Compared to those pebbles, baseballs looked like basketballs coming at me! Good practice does make more perfect if one has the determination to do it. But remember, most children do not have this level of dedication. Very few children will put in the hours of practice as children as did Tiger Woods, Ben Hogan, Barry Bonds, or Ken Griffey, Jr. If your children seem of average talent only, but have the zeal and passion to excel at something, please let them go for it.

Since the human brain is enormously complex, then so is the measurement of the various abilities. So a detailed evaluation is best left to vocational experts. They can determine how your children compare to the general population in aptitudes such as mechanical, mathematical, clerical, memory, social/interpersonal, hand-eye coordination, vision attributes, problem solving, spatial visualization, and many others.

Here's how to proceed: If your school counselors can't do this type of testing—and they probably won't be able to the degree I'm recommending—then get them to recommend either a psychologist or a licensed professional counselor who specializes in vocational testing and counseling, who will administer a battery of ability, vocational, and interest tests to your children. You then want this person to interpret the tests to you and your children, make some recommendations, and write you a summarizing report. Ask for copies of all the tests for future use in higher education or later in life. You may also need a few counseling sessions to augment this process, depending on your children's circumstances. My experience has proven that the best time to do this is about ninth to eleventh grade in high school, but any time is better than not doing it at all.

A word of caution: *Do* make sure that the professional you select has experience in this process with teenagers. Just because one is a licensed counselor or psychologist does not necessarily qualify him or her as an expert in this area. This is the age of specialization, so you want someone trained or experienced specifically in this area. If you have trouble locating someone, contact your state's counseling or psychological licensing board, school officials, or teachers. They should be able put you in touch with the right person.

This process will at least get your children started out with a career roadmap, helping them to successfully negotiate the complex vocational landscape. It will give them in-depth information about themselves, relative to the work world and other areas, and will be enormously useful in making good career decisions for the rest of their lives. Later, as adults, they may want further testing and counseling as the work world changes. The average person changes jobs about ten times and careers five times. With our rapidly changing world economy and job markets, forty years with the same company, with a gold watch at retirement, is no longer the reality in the work world. So your children need to be continually ready for such a job market.

Vocational testing and counseling give your children a cohesive, rational picture of themselves, as they relate to the job market. With this information, they can pick and choose jobs more intelligently, thus having more satisfying vocational lives.

CHAPTER 14

MONEY MANAGEMENT

One of the most important skills your children need to have as adults is the ability to live responsibly on the amount of money they have at their disposal. They will need to know how to live within their means, how to save for the proverbial rainy day, how to make their money compound and grow, how to shop and bargain for things, how to manage a bank account, how to use credit cards, how to save for those special things they want but can't quite afford at the present time, and how to prepare for retirement after their work life is over. It's no secret that many people in America today—our national government included—are in trouble because they have not taken the necessary steps for responsible financial management.

Now, you can't personally teach your children all these things in their early years, nor are they interested in learning about them in childhood, but you can lay the groundwork in their minds so that they will do further research on their own later.

Start off by giving your children a small allowance at around age three or four. Encourage them to put part of it in a piggy bank. Tie the allowance to a chore, such as cleaning their rooms and picking up their toys when they're through playing with them. As they grow older, give them more complex household chores. *Do not* give an allowance with no chores attached, or give too big an allowance. You don't want them to think that money comes easily, especially if they do nothing to earn it. Giving too much tends to develop an inflated sense of worth and entitlement, so use your common sense on the amount to give, based on what your children need at their particular stage of development. Let them spend part of their allowance on any reasonable things they want (1).

As they mature, the allowance should be increased, with the chores becoming more complex. If you live on a farm, they might get the allowance for feeding the chickens and collecting eggs, for instance. Children in the city or suburbs could earn their allowance for watching over their baby brothers or sisters, or raking the yard. You get the idea; this is not calculus.

Of course, parents buy the food and clothing, pay the home's mortgage, etc., but suppose your daughter comes to you and says she wants to take ballet lessons, for example. Now, you may decide to pay for them yourself, and there'd be no harm in that, but this would be a good opportunity to teach a useful lesson. You could say, "Honey, I think that's wonderful. It'll be great exercise and will greatly help your balance, rhythm, and grace. It really pleases me that you want to do something like that. Now, Mommy and Daddy are working hard to save money for your college fund, and since ballet lessons are going to cost thirty dollars each, do you think you could pay for part of them out of your allowance? How much do you think you could pay?"

At this point, your child will be forced to think seriously about how much she really wants to take these lessons, or whatever else it is she is asking to do. If she really wants the lessons, she will likely name a figure, and after some negotiation with you, off she will go to become the next Maria Tallchief, or whoever it is she idolizes.

When my son was in the eleventh grade, he came to his mother and me wanting a car. (Yes, I know you've heard this story, but I'll bet you are not inclined to handle it the way we did.) We agreed that he'd earned the right to drive. (Besides, I was getting tired of driving him to all his high school extracurricular activities and sports practices.) We told him we would think about it. Well, he was impatient and took our need for a contemplative period as a possible strategy to refuse his request, so he came back with a counter offer: He said he'd use his money.

After thinking further, I told him that if he found a suitable car and paid for it himself, then he and I would work on it together to get it in good running shape. I envisioned it as a father-son activity that would draw us closer together, and I could teach him the basics of auto mechanics, which I considered useful to know.

So he went out and, with my advice and assistance, bought a 1982 Ford Escort with a blown head gasket for $270. The car was in good shape, except for the engine, which was the type of vehicle we were looking for. We towed the car home, put it in the garage, and over a several months period, overhauled the engine together, with me paying for the needed parts. Soon he had a serviceable car with a new engine. He used that car for the rest of high school and through college. He now owns new vehicles, and for a while, he changed his own spark plugs, oil, and filters. When he takes his vehicles in for servicing, he knows how to handle that mysterious world of auto repair and service, because he knows what goes on under the hood.

Meanwhile, when all this repair work was going on, my daughter got involved somewhat, and she learned quite a bit herself. As a result, she knows a few things about auto maintenance, which has been of considerable benefit to her.

Teach your children to share their money. Let them know early on that they're expected to put a little something of their own in the collection plate at church or Sunday school. Let them see you do the same. If you give to community charities, tell them about it and why you do it. Teach them to buy presents for their friends and relatives on special occasions, like holidays and birthdays, but also sometimes for no other reason than to just give something to a special person.

You will note that children love to get money as a present. There's something magical about opening an envelope from Granddad and Grandmom and finding a Jackson, a Grant, or a Franklin inside. Getting money this way teaches them that, occasionally, life gives you things of value without having to work for them. This shows children that, occasionally, good things happen without a lot of hard work, and it reduces any tendency to overdo the work bit. Of course, we don't want to do this too often; once in a while is sufficient. I remember some of my aunts and uncles, on rare occasions, giving me money for no reason other than they loved me. And believe me, it made a powerful impression, mainly because my parents didn't have much to give and I had to work hard for any extras. So these extra gifts were exciting treasures—much appreciated. But they didn't happen too often!

On the negative side, if your children have a tendency to be miserly and un-sharing, you must pay even more attention to the above recommendations. Adult misers are not the people to become. They are talked about behind-the-back more than any person I can think of. Miserliness arises from a combination of bad/no training and insecurity. Misers are needless worriers who basically believe the glass is half empty—and has a hole in it! They hoard their money for emergencies that rarely come. Deep down, they believe that security comes from money, not realizing emotionally that real security comes from having a solid, loving network of family and friends, who will be there for them if calamity strikes. Social skills training and continuous positive social interactions all through childhood will usually counter any miserly tendencies that your children might have (2). If this doesn't work, and you can't figure out what else to do, then take your children to a counselor who specializes in working with children.

At some point, your children will need to learn about credit cards, checking and savings accounts, and other money matters. Basically, they need to know that credit cards can get them into considerable debt fast, if not used properly. So, I don't recommend them having a credit card until graduating from high school, and either getting a job or going off to college. For college-bound children, there needs to be some strict guidelines about credit card usage. Of course, they are to be paid off monthly to avoid high interest.

Before high school is over, open up a checking account for your children and let them pay for their various bills with checks or online with the computer. Show them how to write checks and to keep the checkbook balanced. If you're an electronic-banking family, with direct deposit, ATM usage, and the like, show them the monthly statements and explain the details. Also, you can encourage your children to take classes in high school about personal finances, if you think it's necessary.

Take your children on shopping trips and let them see how you select items based on cost and usefulness. Teach them how to select things of good price and quality that will last, as opposed to being cheap and serving only the moment.

The bottom line in all this is it is critical that your children learn how to manage their financial lives. We live in a society where most of our wants and needs involve money in one manner or another. I can't tell you how many clients and friends I've had over the years that were lacking the intellectual and emotional skills necessary to properly manage their everyday monetary affairs. And the life problems this causes seems endless, from going to jail for not paying child support, to being evicted for not paying rent, to spending money on unnecessary things. If you can't manage your personal finances in this country, you've got problems you don't want.

CHAPTER 15

COMPUTER SKILLS

Am I stretching it a bit to say that your children need to have computer skills in order to be successful? Do they need computer skills to be carpenters, mechanics, sales clerks, plumbers, doctors, or like me, counselors? At first glance it would seem not. After all, these vocations don't appear to involve sitting down in front of a computer like a data-entry clerk, or an airline reservationist, or perhaps a bank account manager.

But wait! Carpenters may spend most of their time sawing, measuring, and nailing, but they might have to use a computer to go online to order special materials or prepare bid estimates for jobs. And mechanics, besides installing new spark plugs and changing your oil, had better know how to plug your new car's onboard computer system to computerized diagnostic equipment if they're going to track down the short circuit that keeps fouling up your instrument-panel readings. And sales clerks at the local building supply store will need the computer to locate that special set of Venetian blinds that you saw in *Architectural Digest*, which, of course, they don't have in stock. And plumbers can use special software to lay out the plumbing system in your dream house that's under construction, saving them time and you a lot of money. And doctors can use special software and the Internet to help diagnose the elusive, rare disease that you might have, which other doctors have been unable to diagnose. And your son, the counselor, needs to know what to do when the agency he works for gets rid of his secretary and hands him a laptop computer in substitution and tells him to help even more people!

So it's becoming increasingly clear that almost all jobs require some sort of computer skills. You and I might not like this trend, but that's the way it is. Even a farmer friend of mine has a computer to track commodity prices, telling him when to sell his crops and breed his cows, and performing his complex record keeping and income tax filing. There's just no way for successful people to get away from computers and associated electronic equipment.

The good news about this technological trend is that parents don't have to do much. The school system and childhood inquisitiveness will do it for you. All you have to do is keep a computer in the home for everyone's use and make sure your children take the proper computer courses in school. I recommend the computer be kept in a common area of the home, accessible to all and making it easier for you to monitor your children's computer behavior. If you give them a computer in their bedrooms, some might get too absorbed in it and remove themselves from family interaction. But you'll have to use common sense about this. Also, buy them some decent computer games they can play and provide Internet access so they can explore the electronic world of knowledge.

However, a word of caution: You need to instruct them about the negative aspects of the Internet, especially in the areas of pornography, child molesters, and like-minded perverts who use the Internet for their evil ways. Also, you need to teach them the often-overlooked reality that just because it's on the Internet doesn't necessarily make it factual. There's a lot of tripe and opinions disguised as fact out there. This is similar to the printed word phenomenon, in that if it's in a book it must be true.

Also watch the video games your children play—especially during their preteen years. There's a lot of violence in these games, all promoted in the name of harmless fun, but these violent games can condition a casual attitude about death and destruction that you don't want to see in your children (1).

If you are not well versed in the world of computers, take some introductory courses or make an appointment with an expert to give you advice. Your children's school's computer instructors should also be able to help you with this. Also, you probably have a relative or friend who could help you. Of course, most people learn to use computers on their own, but instruction courses facilitate the process.

Remember, computers are neither good nor bad in a moral sense—they just *are*! But they are a part of our everyday lives, and the goodness they will promote in your children's lives will be the use to which they are put.

EPILOGUE

There seems to be a tendency among many conscientious American parents these days to be a bit too obsessive in raising their children to become supreme achievers. This is illustrated by the Little League coach who pushes his child to excel in those areas in which Dad may have failed, or the inner-city, black kid who practices basketball to the neglect of his studies, with dreams of making it to the NBA.

I have noticed a tendency among conscientious parents to obsess and overdo it. A recent article in the *Wall Street Journal*, by Chinese mother Amy Chu, a professor of law at Yale University, illustrates this point vividly. Mrs. Chu has raised her two daughters pretty much as described in Chapter 7, "Tough Love." As you have seen, I'm all for tough love, but I believe Mrs. Chu has overdone it, all with the goal of producing daughters who make straight A's in school and who master the piano and violin. Her techniques border on the rigidness of Marine Corps basic training, but she seems to have produced two very high-achieving children (1).

We are all familiar with the achievement levels of Asian children in the American school systems. They seem to get a disproportionate number of academic honors, high SAT scores, musical accolades, and other honors. Mrs. Chu has produced what are being called "tiger children" (2). Asian culture seems to be very proficient at producing these "tiger children," and that high-achieving culture still prevails in America—even though these people may have lived here for over a hundred years, as evidenced by the numerous "Chinatowns" and other Asian enclaves in most major American cities. In the world of sports we have none other than Tiger Woods, born of an African American father and a mother from Thailand, both of whom instilled in young Tiger strong Buddhist principles and obsessive golf skill training from the age of three. While Tiger went on to become the best golfer in the world, he was unable to manage his married life successfully. Did his obsessive golf training force him to exclude the other skills in life that he should have developed? I think so.

Here's what it boils down to: Obsessive training in children requires an enormous amount of time. It doesn't matter if the training is in academics, sports, music, social skills—whatever. The point is there is only so much time from birth to age eighteen in which children can devote themselves to the parents' notion of superior achievement. Along with high achievement in a selected area is the fact that it leaves little time to pursue other areas—which typically are neglected. And what are children to do if those undeveloped, neglected areas become necessary for survival. What happens, for example, if a child is extensively trained to become a great violinist—to the neglect of developing many other skills as well—and becomes unable to get a job in a symphony orchestra as an adult, due to the fact that people don't attend symphony concerts like they used to, because modern technology has given the general public many other options for their musical entertainment. I know of many people in situations like this, especially in the music and sports realms.

Let's examine another example. Professor Anders Ericsson, his colleagues, and others have done extensive research that pretty much debunks the notion of born geniuses. They cite case after case that supports the idea that geniuses are made—not born. As they see it, the pathway to becoming a genius at music, mathematics, sports, bridge, chess—literally anything—follows this process: Start the activity around age two, under the continual guidance of an expert, and continue *perfect* practice for at least ten thousand hours until the age of eighteen or so. This is the route that Mozart, Tiger Woods, Thomas Edison, Michael Jordan, Ted Williams, and others followed to achieve greatness in their fields. The research also shows that most of these people do not necessarily have exceptional abilities; they simply outworked everyone. They also are not particularly expert in other areas. For example, Ted Williams devoted himself to golf after retiring from baseball, but despite supreme confidence in himself and much practice, he was only an average golfer at best (3).

All this presents an interesting dilemma: If parents want their children to become the very best in a particular area, it will be at the sacrifice of developing skills in many other needed areas, because there simply won't be enough time if ten thousand plus hours are to be achieved. Conversely, if children are expected to become good in all areas of life, they are likely not to become the best in a particular field—though they will become good in those areas to which they devote as much practice as possible.

But here's the clinker in this whole process: The children have to have the interest, the emotional stamina, and dedication to engage in all this. Very few children come by all this naturally, so the parents have to become severe taskmasters to push the children along. Apparently, that is what Mrs. Chu has done with her daughters. If my parents had forced such high achievement behavior on me, I probably would have rebelled, and kept on rebelling, until I wore them down and they left me alone to do what I wanted. Most kids are like that.

There is currently a child-rearing expert whom I greatly admire, and I believe it would be to your immense benefit to pay attention to him. He is John Rosemond, Ph.D., and he writes a nationally syndicated newspaper column. Look him up.

So follow the guidelines in this book, protect and nurture your children, challenge them in all areas of life, let them explore themselves and the world, support their positive efforts, praise their successes, and tailor your efforts with a lot of common sense.

Good luck!

THE END

ABOUT THE AUTHOR

Joe Wilkins lives in Stone Mountain, Georgia. He is a retired licensed professional counselor and certified rehabilitation counselor, having worked for the State of Georgia as a mental illness and alcohol/drug counselor for thirty years, during which time he maintained a private, general counseling practice. He has a bachelor's degree in psychology and a master's degree in rehabilitation counseling, both from Georgia State University.

Beginning in 1972, he was actively involved in improving mental health services for Georgia citizens. He was a pioneering cofounder of several professional organizations: 1) the Georgia Licensed Professional Counselor's Association, 2) Lutheran Services of Georgia, 3) Stepping Stone Rehabilitation Services, 4) Lutheran Counseling Services, and 5) the Georgia Association of Rehabilitation Residences. He has served in various official positions with these and other similar organizations.

He is a past member of the National Rehabilitation Association, the American Counseling Association, the American Mental Health Counselor's Association, the American Society for Training and Development, the Georgia Rehabilitation Association, the Georgia Rehabilitation Counselor's Association, and the Georgia Licensed Professional Counselor's Association. Since this book is biased toward and stresses traditional family and individual values, it is useful to know that Joe has been married one time, to the same woman, Lorela, since 1968. He has two married children, Deirdre and Darrick, graduates of Georgia Tech and the University of Georgia, respectively. Both partially worked their way through college and now have successful careers in family and business. They were raised following the principles in this book.

In addition to counseling and the human services professions, Joe enjoys his family, friends, church, writing, reading, golf, philosophy, electronics, mechanics, gardening, home maintenance, and most other challenges that life has to offer.

REFERENCES

CHAPTER 1

1) Maslow, A.H., *Motivation and Personality*, Chapter 5 (New York, NY: Harper and Brothers, 1954)

2) Sontag, Frederick, *A Kierkegaard Handbook*, pp. 128-136 (Atlanta, GA: John Knox Press, 1979)

CHAPTER 2

1) White, Robert W., *The Abnormal Personality*, Third Edition, Chapter 3 (New York, NY: The Arnold Press Co., 1964)

2) White, Robert W., *ibid*.

3) Wolfenstein, Martha, "Trends in Infant Care," *American Journal of Orthopsychiatry*, XXIII (1953, pp. 120–130)

4) Wilkins, Joe, Personal Case Experience, Georgia Mental Health Institute (Atlanta, GA, 1972–1985)

5) Stendler, Celia B., "Possible Causes of Over Dependency in Young Children," *Child Development,* 25, pp. 125–146 (1954)

6) Wilkins, Joe, *op.cit*

7) Harlow, H.F., "The Nature of Love," *American Psychologist*, XIII, pp. 673–685 (1958)

8) Gagne, Robert M., *The Conditions of Learning,* Second Edition, Chapter 8 (New York, NY: Holt, Rinehart and Winston, Inc., 1970)

9) Dodson, Fitzhugh, *How to Parent*, p. 47 (New York, NY: New American Library, Signet, 1970)

CHAPTER 3

1) Harvey, O.J., "Conceptual Systems and Attitude Change," pp. 201–226, *Attitude, Ego-Involvement and Change*, Sherif, C.W. and Sherif, M., Eds. (New York, NY: Wiley, 1967)

2) Robinson, Ernest , Lectures, Georgia State University (Atlanta, GA, 1969)

3) Harvey, O.J., *op. cit.*

4) Wilkins, Joe, Personal Case Experience, Georgia Mental Health Institute (Atlanta, GA, 1972–1985)

5) Harvey, O.J., *op. cit.*

6) Harvey, O.J., *op. cit.*

7) Harvey, O.J., *op. cit.*

8) Harvey, O.J., *op.cit.*

CHAPTER 4

1) Patterson, C.H., *Theories of Counseling and Psychology*, Chapter 4, "Rational-Emotive Psychotherapy: Albert Ellis," (New York, NY: Harper & Row, 1966)

2) Papolos, Demitri F., and Papolos, Janice, *Overcoming Depression*, p. 56 (New York, NY, Harper & Row, 1987)

3) Harbison, JoAnn, Personal Case Experience, Georgia Mental Health Institute (Atlanta, GA: 1984)

CHAPTER 5

1) Anonymous psychiatrist, Georgia Occupational Forum, Lecture (Atlanta, GA, 1983)

2) Dodson, Fitzhugh, *How to Parent*, Chap. 6, "Preschool, Part One," (New American Library: Signet, 1970)

3) Dodson, Fitzhugh, *ibid.*

4) Jourard, Sidney M., *Personal Adjustment*, pp. 105–106 (London, England: The MacMillan Co., 1963)

5) Patterson, C.H., *Theories of Counseling and Psychotherapy,* Chapter 4: "Rational-Emotive Therapy: Ellis" (New York, NY: Harper and Row, 1966)

6) Sehnert, Kenneth W., *Stress/Unstress,* Chap. 17, "Exercise: Your Safest Tranquilizer," (Minneapolis, MN: Augsburg Publishing House, 1981)

7) Wilkins, Joe, Personal Case Experience, DeKalb Addiction Clinic (Atlanta GA, 1972–2002)

8) Ayllon, Teodoro and Azrin, Nathan, *The Token Economy,* Chapter 5, "Maximizing the Effectiveness of the Reinforcer," (New York NY: Appleton-Century-Crofts, 1968)

9) Maslow, A.H., *Motivation and Personality,* Chapter 17 (New York, NY: (Harper and Row, 1954)

CHAPTER 6

1) Wilkins, Joe, Personal Case Experience, at the Georgia Mental Health Institute (Atlanta GA, 1980)

2) Jourard, Sidney M., *Personal Adjustment,* Chapter 9, "Interpersonal Behavior and Healthy Personality," (London, England: MacMillan Co., 1963)

3) Alberti, Robert E. and Emmons, Michael L., *Your Perfect Right,* Chapter II (San Luis Obispo, CA: Impact, 1974)

4) Wilkins, Joe, Stepping Stone Rehabilitation Residences (College Park, GA, 1980–2008)

CHAPTER 7

1) Anonymous Authors, *Alcoholics Anonymous*, Chapters 5, 6 and 7 (NewYork,NY: Alcoholics Anonymous World Services, Inc., 1976)

2) Pritchard, Frank, Personal Experience, US Marine Corps (Parris Island, SC, 1968)

CHAPTER 8

1) White, Robert W., *The Abnormal Personality*, Chapter 3 (New York, NY: The Ronald Press, 1964)

2) Wilkins, Joe, Assertiveness Training Therapy, the Georgia Mental Health Institute (Atlanta, GA, 1973-1974)

3) Alberti, Robert E. and Emmons, Michael L., *Your Perfect Right*, Chapter II (San Luis Obispo, CA: Impact, 1974)

4) Alberti, Robert E. and Emmons, Michael L., *ibid.*

5) Alberti, Robert E. and Emmons, Michael L., *ibid.*

6) Alberti, Robert E. and Emmons, Michael L., *ibid.*

7) Alberti, Robert E. and Emmons, Michael L., *Your Perfect Right*, Chapter III, (San Luis Obispo, CA: Impact, 1974)

8) Haddle, Harold and Smits, Stanley, Assertive Skills Training, Georgia State University (Atlanta, GA, 1974)

9) Alberti, Robert E. and Emmons, Michael L., *Your Perfect Right*, p. 83 (San Luis Obispo, CA: Impact, 1974)

CHAPTER 9

1) Adler, Mortimer J., *The Conditions of Philosophy*, p. 244 (New York, NY: Atheneum, 1965)

2) Anonymous, *Alcoholics Anonymous*, Chap. 4, "We Agnostics," (New York, NY: Alcoholics Anonymous World Services, 1976)

CHAPTER 10

1) Trice, Harrison M., and Roman, Paul M., *Spirits and Demons at Work*, pp. 41-43 (Ithaca, N.Y., New York State School of Industrial and Labor Relations, 1972)

2) Wilkins, Joe, Lecture, Emory School of Medicine, VA Program (Atlanta, GA, 1978)

3) National Institute on Alcohol Abuse and Alcoholism, Various Publications (Bethesda, MD,1977–1978)

4) Talbot, G. Douglas, Personal Conversations, DeKalb Addiction Clinic (Atlanta, GA, 1981)

5) Medical Staff Opinions, Georgia Mental Health Institute (Atlanta, GA, 1972–1987)

6) Wilkins, Joe, Unpublished Research, Georgia Department of Human Resources (Atlanta, GA, 1979)

7) Wilkins, Joe, Clinical Experience, Georgia Department of Human Resources (Atlanta, GA, 1972–2002)

8) National Institute on Alcohol Abuse and Alcoholism, Various Publications (Bethesda, MD , 1977-2011)

9) Wilkins, Joe, Clinical Experience, DeKalb Addiction Clinic, (Atlanta, GA, 1973–1975)

CHAPTER 11

1) Kowalski, Robert E., *The 8-Week Cholesterol Cure*, Chap. 7, (New York, NY: Harper & Row, 1987)

2) Pritchard, Frank, Personal Opinion, (Atlanta, GA, 2008)

3) The Food Network, TV Broadcasts, (2009)

4) Stancil, Rosemary and Wilkins, Lorela, *Kids Simply Scrumptious Microwaving* (Atlanta, GA: Kitchen Classics, 1985)

CHAPTER 12

1) Dodson, Fitzhugh, *How to Parent*, Chap. 7 (New York NY: New American Library, 1970

2) Wilkins, Joe Clinical Experience, Georgia Mental Health Institute (Atlanta, GA, 1972–1990)

3) Wilkins, Joe, *ibid.*

4) Wilkins, Joe, *ibid.*

5) *The Weekly Standard*, "The End of Marriage in Scandinavia," www.weeklystandard.com. (January 29, 2011)

6) Wilkins, Joe, Couples Counseling in Private Practice, (Stone Mountain, GA, 1980–2002)

CHAPTER 13

1) Cetron Marvin J., and Appel, Marcia, *Jobs of the Future*, p.1 (New York, NY: McGraw Hill, 1984)

2) Jones, Edward E. and Girard, Harold B *Foundations of Social Psychology*, pp. 22–23 (New York, NY: John Wiley & Sons, 1967)

3) Schonert, Keith W., *Stress/Unstress*, pp. 42–45 (Minneapolis MN: Augsburg Publishing House, 1981)

4) Ayllon, Teodoro and Azrin, Nathan, *The Token Economy*, pp. 1–16 (New York, NY: Appleton-Century-Crofts, 1968)

5) Harbison, JoAnn, Professional Experience, at the Georgia Mental Health Institute (Atlanta, GA, 1974–2000)

6) Harbison, Jo Ann, *ibid*.

CHAPTER 14

1) Ayllon, Teodoro and Azrin, Nathan, *The Token Economy*, Chap. 8 (New York, NY: Appleton-Century-Crofts, 1968)

2) Minwirth, Frank; Newman, Brian; and Warren, Paul; The *Father Book*, pp. 207–209 (Nashville, TN: Thomas Nelson Publishers, 1992)

CHAPTER 15

1) Valentine, C.W., *The Normal Child*, Chap. 12 (Baltimore MD: Penguin Books, 1960)

EPILOGUE

1) Chu, Amy "Why Chinese Mothers Are Superior," *The Wall Street Journal* (New York, NY: January 8–9, 2011)

2) Chu, Amy, *Battle Hymn of the Tiger Mother* (New York, NY: Penguin Press, 2011)

3) Ericsson, K.A., "Expert Performance and Deliberate Practice," (Tallahassee FL, www.psy.fsu.edu/faculty/ericsson.dp.html, 2011)

INDEX

A

Nerds, 33
Nixon, Richard, 1
Non-assertive people, 125

O

Obsessive child rearing, 221
Only child, 64
Organized churches, 144
Over-empowerment, 105-107

P

Parental authority, 48-50
Parole boards, 113
Passive-aggressive behavior, 54, 117
Passive child, 50
Peer relationships, 94-97, 147, 196-197
Percentages of success, 65, 73
Perfect children, 5
Personal appearance, 74
Physical activity, 62, 89-90, 164-167
Physical needs, infants, 8
Political persuasions, 22
Poor teachers, dealing with, 98-100
Positive self-image, infants, 8-9
Positive thinking, 60
Prisoners, 113
Problem solving, 32

T

W

Made in the USA
Columbia, SC
14 August 2021

42784398R00146